Unscripted

Unscripted

CONVERSATIONS ON LIFE AND CINEMA

VIDHU VINOD CHOPRA

WITH ABHIJAT JOSHI

EDITED BY NASREEN MUNNI KABIR

EBURY
PRESS

An imprint of Penguin Random House

EBURY PRESS

USA | Canada | UK | Ireland | Australia
New Zealand | India | South Africa | China

Ebury Press is part of the Penguin Random House group of companies
whose addresses can be found at global.penguinrandomhouse.com

Published by Penguin Random House India Pvt. Ltd
7th Floor, Infinity Tower C, DLF Cyber City,
Gurgaon 122 002, Haryana, India

Penguin
Random House
India

First published in Ebury Press by Penguin Random House India 2021

ISBN 9780670094585

Typeset in Helvetica Neue by Manipal Technologies Limited, Manipal
Printed at Replika Press Pvt. Ltd, India

www.penguin.co.in

Dedicated
to all those in small towns
who have big dreams

Foreword

Zuni Chopra

In many ways, I do not know the man you will meet in these pages. An interesting complex that every child must grapple with; for in the end, we have seen little more than a quarter of our parents' lives, though they have seen all of ours. They have known every shard of our newborn souls, raw and slow-changing, and we have only known their world as they have crafted it for us. But in many ways, the gaze of a child runs deeper than the doting of a parent. We see you, always, for what you are, no matter the erosion of time and the desperate shielding of protective love. So here I am, a freshly fallen acorn, proud to tell you of the mighty oak from which I came, astonished upon falling to realize that I had only ever truly beheld the single branch that bore me.

My father. Gosh. I don't know if it's possible to fit a man of such enormous character and such powerful spirit into the confines of a few small letters. He has taught me far more than he knows. He moves like a river, passing over the largest boulders with a surety of current and a powerful rush. He believes in himself, and his family, and his cinema, and little else. He chases self-defined excellence, he dreams of creating art; art painted on the canvas of a silver screen, beyond the mindless popcorn spectacle. He relishes each moment of life as he does each bite of dinner, never letting any blockbuster or box-office failure distract him in his fundamental joy. Unbreakable in his core values; for happiness without integrity is no happiness at all. I have seen his generosity change lives; I have seen his wisdom transform those close to him; I have seen his ever-enduring courage lift up those who need it most. If we have so much to give, he says, why don't we? You will only fly as high as your confidence takes you, and you are worth far more than you can imagine. That is what he has taught me. And now, he has bound his lifetime into this book's beaming binding, and I hope sincerely that you will unearth your own fragments of faith and morsels of courage from between the lines of its freshly inked stories. I hope that my father can give you the hope he has always given me. After all, this is the man who will someday burst into heaven and challenge God to turn him down.

DOLPHIN MOMENTS

Abhijat Joshi

I met Vidhu Vinod Chopra twenty-six years ago, when I was twenty-six. So I've known him for exactly half my life.

My first play, *A Shaft of Sunlight*, had won an award at the BBC World Service Playwriting Contest, and was being performed at the Birmingham Repertory Theatre. Vinod saw the play in Birmingham and liked it, inquired about the playwright, and left instructions that I should meet him when in Mumbai. I was visiting Paris at that time, thanks to the money earned from the play. Vinod may have assumed I was older than I was, educated in the USA or UK, polished. If so, he did not show his surprise when he met a young, bumbling playwright from Ahmedabad with a small-town sensibility.

That meeting from twenty-six years ago, in Vinod's small apartment in Bandra, is as fresh and vivid in my memory as if it had happened yesterday. Everything that defines Vinod, with all his charm and flaws and capacity for greatness, was on display in those few hours. Here is a list of the most striking things:

1. Vinod told me my play was the most brilliant piece of theatre he had seen for a long, long time. The same evening, with the same conviction, he also told me that my play was 'quite average', barring some flashes of good writing here and there. This made him believe he could train me.

2. He told me that as India's best director, he actually deserved and desired to work with a playwright like Tom Stoppard. But for the moment, I would do. A little later, he said with equal sincerity he had no interest in the kind of wordplay that Tom Stoppard indulged in, and Stoppard could actually never dream of attaining the intensity and poignancy of my play. ('Stoppard ka baap nahin likh sakta.')

3. He told me to quit my job as a college lecturer with immediate effect and help with his new script, and said he would match my salary, which was 6,000 rupees a month. When I declined to do so on the grounds that I liked teaching, he lauded the decision, spoke movingly about his teacher Ritwik Ghatak, expressed the hope that I would not get corrupted in Mumbai, and assured me he'd throw me out once I did. 'Once', not if!

4. He poured me my first-ever single malt and treated me to the best meal I had ever eaten. He quoted freely from Kahlil Gibran and Ghalib while eating with relish, and spoke about Kashmir and his father.

5. He showed me Ingmar Bergman's three commandments on his soft board: 'Thou shalt entertain, thou shalt not sell thy soul while entertaining, and thou shall treat each

film as if it is your last film.' He enunciated them with such fervour that I felt he was trying to chisel them on to my mind.

6. He uttered two Vinodesque proclamations I found enthralling. The first was, 'Write a film for Bertrand Russell, but for God's sake don't bore him.' The other was, 'Write a film you want to see, don't try to guess what others may want to see. Because if the film flops, there would be at least one person in the world who likes it: and that's you.'

7. As I was leaving, he asked me if I could extend my stay in Mumbai for a few more days before leaving for Ahmedabad, to try some writing. I immediately agreed. He promised he'd pick up my hotel bill, and later did.

8. He gave me a VCR to take back with me to Ahmedabad when he learnt I did not possess one. He said I must immediately watch *Citizen Kane, 8½, All That Jazz, The Godfather* and Kurosawa's *Red Beard*. He told me I'd feel tremendously inspired by those films. And if I wasn't, he said, 'You needn't come back here to write. It wouldn't be worth even trying.'

When I returned to the hotel, I was intrigued, charmed, exhausted, confused. I could not put this man in any bracket. He was unlike anyone I had ever met. His arrogance bordered on rudeness, but he was genuinely humble while remembering Ritwik Ghatak. Even more so while expressing his awe of *Citizen Kane*. He said his own films were nothing but certain specific kind of hair in the human anatomy compared to Welles's masterpiece. There was a zany innocence to his contradictions about Tom Stoppard. His joy was infectious while he drank, ate and quoted Ghalib. His passion for cinema was real, fierce and motivating. But what set him apart completely were the two gestures—giving me the VCR, and offering to pay my hotel bill. The first told me he really wanted me to learn, keen that my raw talent not die without nurture and exposure. The second told me he did not live in an ivory tower, he understood and cared about the realities of his associates. With those two gestures, he was already beginning to look after me. Already becoming a bit of the elder brother that he later became. Already pulling me into what he calls his 'cinema family'.

Vinod, above all, is the quintessential family man. He is happy when his family is happy. In the last twenty-six years, I don't know a single day when he isn't tackling someone's problem—someone from his staff, friends, relatives, colleagues. His blood family, or his cinema family. The troubles can range from someone's landlord to another's brain surgery. A part of Vinod's mind seeks practical solutions throughout the day; the other part seeks creative solutions for the snags in the film he's directing. For the first set of problems he makes phone calls to doctors, lawyers, police officers from his vast circle of friends. For the second set of problems he musters help from Kurosawa, Welles or Hitchcock. He tries to end his usually eventful days around 8 p.m., and then like Luis Buñuel, who said he never missed a cocktail in his adult life, tries not to miss his single malt, or wine or Beluga. After that, over dinner, he loves to boast about how well he did during the day to

Anupama (theirs is undoubtedly the best marriage I have seen in my life) and his brilliant, talented children. They react with gentle humour, pricking his ego now and then, loving him as fiercely as he loves them. From each day, no matter how tough, he manages to find something to be hopeful about, and thanks 'Bhagwaan-ji' for his good fortune before going to sleep.

This is the rhythm of Vinod's average day.

Then there are days that bring 'Dolphin Moments'.

This phrase entered our lives a few years ago through Vinod's elder brother Vir Chopra. Vir-ji spends a part of the year among the bluest waters and the sunniest isles of the Maldives for business. Every evening in that tranquil land seems straight out of a Wordsworth poem: 'It's a beauteous evening, calm and free. The holy time is quiet as a nun . . .' But one day, Vinod received a call from Vir-ji, who was almost shouting with excitement: 'Vinod! I have come to a small island, and would you believe it? There are hundreds of dolphins around me. My God! This is unreal. They are singing . . .' Vir-ji, a quiet and dignified gentleman, was so moved by this sight that he could not contain the joy he felt. He had to share it. We started calling this phenomenon the 'dolphin moments'. Moments which are so intense that they provide a heightened sense of being alive. They stay vivid and immediate in the memory long after they pass.

My first such moment with Vinod was in 1995 when he made me open a bottle of champagne when I heard I was going to be a father. It was the first champagne bottle I held in my hand, and as I nervously fiddled with it, the cork flew out of the balcony. Vinod dispatched me to find it. I retrieved it from the laundry shop downstairs. He and I signed that cork to mark the moment. Since then there has been a cavalcade of dolphin moments, and corresponding corks: Walking up Summit Drive in LA in search of Chaplin's house; meeting the great actor Peter O'Toole on a plane and then having him over for dinner (that day I witnessed the boy from Srinagar in Vinod, looking at Sir David Lean through the lens of O'Toole); listening for hours to Werner Herzog's intense anecdotes (that day I witnessed the film school student Vinod, speaking far less than he listened); getting mesmerized by Amitabh Bachchan Saab reciting his father's poems for hours on 5 September 2015; Vinod calling me from Bertolt Brecht's statue in Berlin; I calling him from Ghalib's house in Ballimaran and from Ghalib's mazaar in Nizamuddin; his calling me from Michelangelo and Galileo's tombs in Florence; my getting drunk on his birthday in 2010 and his forbidding me to take the flight back to Ahmedabad and my assuring him it would be the pilot and not I who'd be flying the plane (Raju has recorded parts of this evening); his arranging the first-ever screening of *3 Idiots* for Sachin Tendulkar, and allowing me to introduce the film knowing what Sachin meant to me; celebrating the opening night of *Lage Raho Munna Bhai* with Raju and the team with thirteen bottles of Dom Perignon that Bachchan Saab so generously sent, perhaps emptying out his cellar . . .

The book you're about to read is mostly a recounting of the dolphin moments in Vinod's life. Over the last twenty-six years he narrated to me, mostly in the context of writing our scripts, hundreds of moments that were unforgettable due to their drama or poignancy or humour.

All I did during our conversations was to take him back to those moments. Nasreen Munni Kabir has done an incredible job of giving a shape and form and flow to these free-ranging memories, making this book possible. Most of these moments are from the period when he was a struggler, a rebel. I hope they will inspire a film student, and entertain a reader who likes but is not necessarily wedded to films.

I shall end with a dolphin moment so huge that I must coin a new phrase and call it a 'whale moment'. The circumstances that brought about this moment were grim. Soon after *Lage Raho Munna Bhai* was released, my father suffered a massive stroke in Ahmedabad. A couple of days later, a courier arrived for me from Mumbai. It carried my remuneration for the film. I was grateful for the timing, as the money was needed to pay for the hospital treatment. In 2006, something between 8 and 12 lakhs was considered good fees for a film script. Knowing Vinod's tremendous enthusiasm for the 'Lage Raho' script, I gathered I'd be paid more than what I was due. But I was not prepared for what emerged from the envelope. It was a cheque for one crore—equivalent of 6–7 crores today. (Much later I learnt, when the accounts section told Vinod the cheque should be of 90 lakhs, because 10 lakhs had to be deducted at source as tax, he raised the amount to 1 crore 10 lakhs. He wanted to be sure the cheque I would show my father would have the words one crore on it.)

Instead of trying to describe what happened next, I would like to convey it through excerpts from an email I sent Vinod that evening:

Monday, December 04, 2006 5:26 PM

Dear Vinod,

The cheque arrived, and I failed to accomplish the simple task of calling you . . . If I were a religious man, I would have performed some sacred ritual . . . I sat numbly for a few minutes, and thought about what you and this film have done for my life. Then I took it to my father in the hospital. For the first time since his hospitalization, he summoned his glasses. He looked at the cheque, and looked at it again, focused hard to try and see it. Then he murmured, 'Class . . . class . . .' Obviously he was paying tribute to your incredibly grand gesture. He had seen too much of life to not realize that most people don't do this . . .

Tears were forced back, but I am sure they were shed once I left. A teacher's son, who is also a teacher, does not receive rewards like this.

Your father wouldn't have been able to believe you could give away cheques like this. My father can't believe I received one like this.

I couldn't call. I can't write either. So I will just stop . . .

Love,
Abhijat.

Like in the email, I should stop writing here. Because if this gesture of his does not tell what Vidhu Vinod Chopra is, whatever else I might write, cannot. As Vinod said to me in our first meeting, 'It wouldn't be worth even trying.'

THE CONVERSATION

Abhijat Joshi [AJ]: According to the great French film-maker Jean-Luc Godard, a film must have a beginning, middle and end and not necessarily in that order! I think it's the pattern we should follow in this book. We've known each other too long to have a linear, straightjacketed conversation. I'm sure you'll agree.

Vidhu Vinod Chopra [VVC]: I'm in your hands, Mr Joshi. [*smiles*]

AJ: Whenever we've talked you have said how amazed you are to have fulfilled your dreams of making films—given that you came from a small mohalla in Kashmir and succeeding in films was quite an unlikely feat.

Personally, I'm not that amazed because your work stood out from the very start. Your first film, *Murder at Monkey Hill*, in which you also played the lead role, was a slick crime thriller but most unusually, as the film reached the climax, you abruptly ended the story by citing the fact that you had run out of film stock! I thought it was a very bold way to highlight the inadequate resources available to young film-makers.

And then, *Murder at Monkey Hill* went on to win you a National Award in 1976. But the 24th National Films Award ceremony did not go as planned, did it? [*both laugh*]

VVC: No, it didn't. I was told I'd receive a prize money of 4000 rupees along with the National Award for the Best Short Experimental Film. I was very excited and went to Delhi for the ceremony. When my name was called, I went onto the stage where President Neelam Sanjiva Reddy and Mr L.K. Advani, the Minister for Information and Broadcasting, were standing. The President hung a red silk band with a gold medallion around my neck and handed me a brown official-looking envelope. I expected to find 4000 rupees in it, but when I opened the envelope, instead of bank notes, out comes a postal bond cashable in seven years with a note saying I'd get double the money seven years later, or some shit like that.

I just stood there staring at Mr Advani. Our exchange went something like this:

Sir! This is not money. This is a bond.
Yes, yes, it's money. You'll get it later.
No, sir! But you promised me cash. This is a bond.

There I was talking to a minister like that on the stage of Vigyan Bhawan. Mr L.K. Advani got irritated and tried to calm me down:

Okay, meet me tomorrow, we'll sort it out. Don't worry.
No, sir. If I get off this stage, I know I won't be able to reach you tomorrow.
But this is a bond. It'll be good for you.
Sir, you keep the bond and give me the 4000 in cash.

Watching our argument unfold, President Reddy asked me what was going on and I blurted out: 'Sir! This gentleman promised me cash and he's giving me a bond saying I should go now. I know if I get off this stage, nothing will happen. I'll be done for!'

By this time, Mr Advani had lost his temper and spoke firmly:

I'm telling you. Come to Shastri Bhawan at eleven o'clock tomorrow.
You'll give me the money then, sir?
Yes! I'll give you the money.

I turned to the President and said:

Sir, there are only three people on this stage. You, him and me. Can I come to you if he doesn't give me the money?
Yes, yes. Mr Advani is a minister, and if he tells you he'll give it to you, he will. If he doesn't, call me. We'll help you.

I finally got off that damn stage. I later heard from someone that this entire interaction was telecast live on Doordarshan.

At eleven o'clock the next day I made my way to Shastri Bhawan. I had never seen a room as large as Mr Advani's. He sat behind his desk looking furious. My God, was he angry! He looked at me and moved the phone on his desk towards me and said in crisp Hindi:

Apne pitaji ko phone lagaaiye. [Call your father.] Is this the future India I'm seeing? Is this it? You speak to me like that in front of the President? For 4000 rupees? Call your father right now.

Pitaji Kashmir mein hain. Aap baat kar lijiye. 337 . . . [My father is in Kashmir. Please talk to him, sir. His number is 337 . . .]

As he was dialling the number, I couldn't control myself and said:

Have you had your breakfast, sir?

It's 11. Yes, I've had breakfast.

I haven't. And I'm hungry because I don't have any money. This shirt I'm wearing cost me sixty rupees and I wore it for the first time for the National Awards ceremony. I usually travel third class, but I came to Delhi in an air-conditioned chair-car compartment. The ticket cost over 200 rupees. I also borrowed 1200 rupees from my friends thinking I'd be getting 4000 in cash and I'd return the money to them. Now what can I tell them? They'll get double the money in seven years? Yesterday you promised me the cash in front of the President. If you won't give it to me, I'll go and see him.

He put down the telephone receiver, gave me a long look and asked:

You haven't had your breakfast? So what will you have?

Eggs and a paratha.

He picked up the phone and ordered breakfast for 'Vinod-ji'. He became a different man after that and arranged that I be given rupees 4000 in cash immediately. Since that day, Mr L.K. Advani became a father figure to me.

Years later, he watched *Shikara* with me at a private screening and was, in fact, one of the first people in Delhi to see the film. He wept when he saw it. I was so touched and grateful.

AJ: The National Awards ceremony story is my all-time favourite.

Your next film, *An Encounter with Faces* (1978), not only won awards in India, but was nominated for an Oscar in 1979 in the Documentary Short Subject category. It's a very moving film about an orphanage, and I'm sad to say, it's still so relevant. When I saw it again on YouTube recently I was struck by the first shot. How did you do that?

VVC: You mean the shot coming into the railway station? The cameraman refused to take the shot so I did it myself. I handheld the Arriflex 2c 35mm camera and rotated it. Once the train pulled into the station, I ran after the kid onto the platform—so the movement was continuous—it was all in one shot.

AJ: It's a great opening.

VVC: *An Encounter with Faces* won many honours, including the Golden Peacock Award at the International Film Festival of India held in Delhi on 16 January 1979. The

Best Short Film Award was given to me by the great Polish director Krzysztof Zanussi. The event was widely covered by the press with write-ups and photographs.

Abhijat, let me tell you something more about Mr L.K. Advani's kindness towards me. He knew I was not well off, so after I had left the FTII, he made me a member on the FTII Governing Council. My airfare to attend the meetings was paid, and so for many months I lived on that airfare—880 rupees. I would save the airfare and buy a third-class ticket and travel by train.

Once I was appointed on the Governing Council, they discovered I was not even an FTII graduate. I had not passed my final exams because some teachers didn't like me. In their opinion, I was arrogant and outspoken and not a particularly good student. I was good at making films but poor when it came to submitting papers. When I got appointed a GC member, the FTII staff objected because I had failed the finals. That's when they decided to give me the diploma. So I got my diploma two years after I had actually left the film institute. By that time I had won several awards for my short films, including an Oscar nomination.

AJ: Why were you regarded as too outspoken? Was it your honesty that led to the spat with your tutors?

VVC: Maybe. It's important for me to be honest—even though it was often inconvenient. I wanted to shape my own life and have never knowingly compromised while expressing my thoughts or making movies. I may make a bad film but it never crossed my mind to make a dishonest one just because it might make money.

AJ: Did that have something to do with the way your father thought?

VVC: Probably yes. He once told me: 'I have no problem if you become a cobbler in our narrow lane, but you must be the best cobbler.' On that same day, he told me a story that had a great impact on me.

There was once a great saint in Kashmir who lived in the nearby hills. The legend goes that one day the ruling maharaja, riding his horse, went to meet the sadhu. He found the saint sitting on a rock enjoying the wintry sun. The maharaja did not dismount and from where he sat, he addressed the sadhu: 'I have heard many things about you, Swami-ji. Please tell me what I can do for you. Can I build an ashram for you? Just say the word and you can have anything you want.'

The sadhu looked up and could only see the silhouette of the maharaja against the bright sunlight. The sadhu said: 'My friend, you're blocking the sun falling on me. Could you please move a little?'

The maharaja immediately got off his horse and moved away. He repeated once again: 'Swami-ji, please tell me what I can do for you.'

The saint smiled and said: 'You have done what I wanted. There's nothing more I want.'

'But you have asked nothing of me.'

'Yes, I have. You were stopping the sunlight from falling on me and when I asked you to move away, you did. Now I can feel the wintry sun on me again. There's nothing more that I want.'

The story makes me realize that little things can make you so happy . . . they are what is really important. All the saint wanted at that moment was to enjoy the soft sun on him.

We actually need very little in life. But we think we need all kinds of things—fashionable brands, luxury items, etc., etc. Finally, a shoe is a shoe. Those material needs just destroy our innocence and our ability to be happy. Greed destroys our peace of mind.

I feel ultimately it's only your work that counts and the good people who lent you a hand along the way.

AJ: You have spoken about those who helped you and recognized your talent early on.

VVC: I remember them all. For instance, Mr V.S. Shastri, the director general of Bombay Doordarshan. He was instrumental in changing my life. He had seen *Murder at Monkey Hill* because I had won the Guru Dutt Memorial Award for the Best Student Film in 1976 and he happened to be on the jury.

One day he was talking about my film in a Doordarshan editing room where my then wife, Renu Saluja, was editing. She had a short-term contract working on a very popular English-language DD series for children called *Magic Lamp* that was being revived and directed by Shukla Das. Renu was paid 330 rupees every fortnight. So when she heard Mr Shastri raving about *Murder at Monkey Hill*, she got very excited and asked him:

Would you like to meet the film's director?
Yes! Do you know him?

Of course, Renu did not say she was married to me, she just said she knew me and would ask me to come and see him. That evening Renu came home thrilled and told me about what had happened.

At our first meeting at the Bombay Doordarshan offices in Worli, Mr V.S. Shastri said: 'I can't pay you very much. But I can give you 2500 rupees to direct, 500 for the screenplay, 500 for dialogue, 500 for costumes and 500 for art direction. A total of Rs 4500. Make whatever you like for us. I'll give you the equipment and a car to travel in.'

I got the shock of my life when I heard him. Here was a man of authority telling me I had free rein to make films the way I wanted to make them. Was my luck turning? I had to be sure I heard him right and asked:

Can I make any film I want?
Anything.
You will not tell me what to do? I will not need to get approval?
No one will need to approve your work.

I couldn't believe it. I thought here was my chance to make a film for DD on my own terms and I no longer needed to make that film I had been planning to make with Amitabh Bachchan.

AJ: So you met Mr Shastri when you and Mr Bachchan were discussing working together on a script that you were writing called *Prashant*? I remember you telling me once that you had met Mr Bachchan earlier thanks to Hrishikesh Mukherjee.

VVC: That's right. The idea of working with Amitabh Bachchan was at the top of every Indian film-maker's wish list. We all knew he was a great actor, and in the 1970s, he was India's biggest superstar.

I made a wish list during a visit to Mahabaleshwar with Renu. She and I had decided to spend some time together there to figure out how we were going to find work in films. There were directors I wanted to assist like Hrishikesh Mukherjee, Basu Chatterjee and Rajinder Singh Bedi. But in the end I never worked as an assistant director. The last name on my wish list was the Films Division and that's exactly where I ended up working! *Encounter with Faces* was made for them—that's the short that got nominated for an Oscar.

Coming back to Amitabh Bachchan. He was number one on my wish list and number two was Sanjeev Kumar. Let me first tell you how I met Mr Bachchan.

I left the film institute around 1976–77 and headed to Bombay. I have always aimed high and knew the only way I could meet Mr Bachchan was through Hrishida. I went to see him with this agenda in mind. I thought I'd ask Hrishida to see *Murder at Monkey Hill* and if he liked the film, I could then request him to introduce me to Mr Bachchan.

I was pretty cocky to think I could work with the top guy in Indian film right off the bat. But luck was on my side. Hrishida saw *Murder at Monkey Hill* and was impressed and so I could pop the question. Magnanimously, Hrishida told me that Mr Bachchan and Rekha were shooting for his film *Alaap* at Mohan Studio the next day, adding, 'Come to my set tomorrow and I'll introduce you.'

I played the innocent, though I knew full well that Mr Bachchan would be at Mohan Studio the next day. I had it all planned!

My brother Ramanand Sagar's office was at Natraj Studio in Andheri, so the next morning I booked the viewing theatre at Natraj from nine to six. I threaded my film in the projector so that if Mr Bachchan agreed to see it, we'd just have to press a button and the film would roll. I did not want to waste time. Natraj was very close to Mohan Studio, so travelling between the two studios would only take a few minutes. I was all fired up and ready for my big moment, but when I arrived at Mohan Studio, I realized all I could do was to wait, and that too, for hours and hours without a sign of Mr Bachchan.

Hrishida had an assistant called Bimalda and he finally took me to meet the great star who was making his way from the set to his make-up room. Amitabh had to climb two steps to enter the make-up room and when he was on the second step, he turned around to talk to me. We all know he's a tall man but standing on the step made him appear even taller—I thought I was looking at a god, you know! [*both smile*]

Bimalda introduced me to Mr Bachchan, and because Bimalda knew I hated being introduced as Ramanand Sagar's brother, he mumbled something and Amitabh misheard him and asked: 'Oh! So he's Vinod Khanna's brother?'

By then I was getting irritated, I shook his hand and said: 'My name is Vinod Chopra. I know it's a terrible name. Very unimpressive. But it's all I have. I've made a short movie, it's only twenty minutes long. You can see it five minutes away from here at Natraj Studio. The film is threaded in the projector and I've booked the theatre from nine to six. If you see my film our introduction will be complete.'

Mr Bachchan was taken aback and asked where we were supposed to see the film. I repeated the business about Natraj Studio, etc. While I was talking, Bimalda did not open his mouth! Mr Bachchan said he would see the film and then stepped into his make-up room and closed the door behind him. Bimalda's expression suggested that he thought I was a lunatic.

I went back to Hrishida's set and the waiting began all over again. It was around three-thirty in the afternoon when another assistant, Bharat Rangachary, came to me and said: 'You're standing here in this dark corner? Bachchan sir won't even notice you're here.' I explained I did not want to appear too pushy and if I could not make my presence felt, how would I be able to direct this big star?

Suddenly at four o'clock there was an uproar on the set. Rekha breaks down, Hrishida shouts. I don't know what was going on but something had happened and Rekha walked off. I thought to myself, 'Shit! That's the end of my screening.' At around 5 p.m., I asked Hrishida what to do. He said: 'You'll have to show him your film some other day.'

Something told me not to give up, so I went back to the unlit corner of the set and sat down. I did not have the money to hire the viewing theatre at Natraj Studio for another day, so I was worried and deeply disappointed.

Close to 6 p.m., I felt this firm hand on my shoulder, I turned around and it was Amitabh Bachchan. In his deep baritone voice, he asked, 'You said the theatre was booked till six, right? Let's go!' I jumped to my feet and we walked towards his van. I could feel the eyes of Hrishida's crew on me. I pretended to be cool, but inside I was shaking with a mix of pride, humility and nervousness. After all, this was Amitabh Bachchan I was walking behind! While making our way to his van, he said:

Is it okay with you if I bring a friend along?
Of course, sir. Anybody, anybody!

I entered the small trailer he used for travelling from set to set. I think everybody in films, and perhaps everyone in Bombay, knew it was his trailer. As we walked in, I saw Rekha sitting there.

AJ: I think you asked him if there was a toilet in the van.

VVC: Remember how fascinated I was with his van, yaar? His van was legendary. I asked if I could use the toilet. It was the high point of my life—taking a leak in Amitabh Bachchan's moving van. [*both laugh*]

A few minutes later, we drove the short distance from Mohan Studio to Natraj. Once they were comfortably settled in their seats, I started the projector and *Murder at Monkey Hill* began.

The film had a split-screen effect at the beginning and Rekha asked me how I did that shot. It really annoyed me, because I wanted Mr Bachchan to watch in silence. I was a bit curt and said: 'Let's please talk at the end of the film.' When the film was over, we stepped out of the theatre and I'll never forget the first thing Mr Bachchan said: 'So when do we work together?'

I was flabbergasted. It felt like many dreams had come true all at once. I started laughing out of nervousness. He stared at me, not sure why I was laughing. He asked what was wrong and I said shakily, 'Sir, my struggle is over.'

I was over the moon. My euphoria lasted for about two and a half days. That's how I met Amitabh Bachchan for the first time.

AJ: Once Mr Shastri said you could make any film you wanted for DD, did you have to go back to tell Mr Bachchan about your job offer?

VVC: Yes. I don't remember if I slept the night before, but first thing the next day, I headed towards Mohan

Studios in the Ambassador car that was assigned to me by Mr Shastri. I felt so proud to be sitting in that white Ambassador because I thought it was my talent and ability as a film-maker that had made it possible.

I was on top of the world and in my excitement, I don't know what I said to Mr Bachchan, but I probably sounded crazy because he was confused: 'What? DD? You mean Kaka? Kaka is hiring you?'

Kaka was what Rajesh Khanna, the other reigning superstar, was affectionately called by the whole film industry. I realized I was not being clear and that's why he thought Rajesh Khanna was going to hire me, so I politely corrected him:

No, not Kaka, sir. I want to make a film for television. DD.
DD? What's DD?

Kids today would not believe it, but there was a time when we weren't familiar with television at all. We had only one channel in India, the state-run black-and-white Doordarshan, in short DD.

I explained to Mr Bachchan that I had been offered a job at Doordarshan and therefore I could not pursue our project of *Prashant*. I said:

Sir, they've made me an offer I can't refuse. They said I can make any film I want.
But you can make any film you want with me.
Not really, sir. If you and I have a difference of opinion, your opinion will matter, not mine. I'm a nobody.

He understood what I was saying but deep down I knew he was angry. I don't know if he had guessed that my real reason for accepting the DD offer came from my desire to be a free spirit. That really mattered to me. Anyway, he probably figured I was completely crazy because nobody in their right mind would give up the chance of working with him.

AJ: What were the films you made for Doordarshan?

VVC: Thanks to Mr Shastri, I made two short films: *Woman* and *Satya Katha*.

Woman was one of the first Indian films made on domestic violence. When the great Urdu writer Ismat Chughtai saw it, she liked it so much that before it played on DD, she spoke about the film and introduced me on air as a young writer-director.

The story of *Woman* revolved around a married couple played by Om Puri and Radha Saluja. The husband is insistent that his wife learn how to cook. She doesn't like him nagging her. At one point, he even slaps her. I used the metaphor of a pressure cooker . . . the increasing oppression of the woman was like the rising pressure in a pressure cooker. By the end of the film, she has no fight left in her. When her husband comes home one evening, she serves him dinner. He's very pleased and asks how she has at last managed to learn how to cook. She answers him in a broken and docile voice: 'Har cheez seekhne mein thoda waqt toh lagta hai.' [Lessons take a little time to learn.]

AJ: That's very moving. What about the story of *Satya Katha*?

VVC: It's the story of a dying beggar and a cop. Naseeruddin Shah plays a cop who wants to help this beggar but is unable to. Ironically, the only thing he can ultimately do for the beggar is to remove his body from the street when he dies.

AJ: Did you write these stories?

VVC: Yes. I remember Raj Kapoor called Renu and me after seeing *Satya Katha* and offered us work, but we were reluctant. We wanted to find our own voice. You know I'd love to see those films again but I'm told the prints are lost, so that's that.

During the time I was making these movies, my parents had come to Bombay from Kashmir to see me. They were happy I had a job and were keen to meet Mr Shastri. I took them to his office and my father asked him: 'I came to meet you only to ask one question. Aap aise paagalon ko filmen banaane kaise dete hain?' [How do you let crazy people like him make films?]

It was my father's idea of a joke. Mr Shastri was an introverted and cultured gentleman and so he graciously replied: 'Crazy people are the ones who can create something special.'

My mother was very upset with my father for asking such a question and I remember she refused to talk to him for days.

V.S. Shastri's attitude to life was something worth learning. He always believed we should do our best and that things would ultimately fall into place. That's what I learnt as a young man—strive for excellence and success follows. It became the motto of my film company: 'Strive for excellence.'

AJ: The contacts you made thanks to *Murder at Monkey Hill* didn't end there. What about your encounter with the producer N.N. Sippy?

VVC: This book would be impossible without you, Abhijat. You remember everything!

Mr N.N. Sippy and his son Pravesh Sippy had seen and liked *Murder at Monkey Hill*. He was a top producer at the time and the god of different cinema—what you might call 'indie' cinema. N.N. Sippy produced many films by Hrishikesh Mukherjee. He asked me to meet him in a restaurant at the Oberoi at Nariman Point.

We FTII students were always broke. And whenever we could eat out, we'd have a meal at the Café Goodluck in the Deccan Gymkhana area of Pune. We never looked at the choice of dishes on the menu; instead, we studied the prices and always ordered the cheapest dishes they had. I think you could get bheja fry for one rupee twenty paise— it was the least expensive mutton dish on the menu and that's what we ate. If we had a bit more cash, we ordered chicken with eggs.

When N.N. Sippy invited me to this fancy restaurant, I did exactly what I used to do at the Café Goodluck.

I didn't look at the choice of dishes, I studied the price of the dishes and ordered the most expensive thing on the menu. It happened to be a lobster curry, but I had never eaten lobster in my life and didn't like the taste of it at all. So I left it untouched.

N.N. Sippy praised my film and said he was interested in working with me. I heard him out and said:

Thank you, sir. But I must have creative freedom and the final say on how the film will turn out.
That's not possible. I have final say. I'm the producer.

That was the end of that conversation! As we were leaving the restaurant, I asked him if he could drop me on the way. During the car ride, no one said a word. I could tell he was really pissed off with me. I'm sure he would've liked to throw me out of the car but instead he was kind enough to drop me at Churchgate railway station. From Churchgate I took a train to Dadar and went to see Manmohan Shetty. He was the owner of Adlabs and he knew I was going to see N.N. Sippy. Manmohan Shetty was a friend and supporter and was very excited that I was meeting a mainstream producer—he thought perhaps this was the break I needed.

What happened?
I had a great meal, ate all sorts of weird things.
But what happened?
He didn't give me full creative control, so I said no to their film.

I will never forget Manmohan Shetty's expression. He looked at me in shock and said: 'Vinod, you're completely broke. You have nothing. The only thing you have is balls! How will you survive?'

I was still hungry because I couldn't eat the lobster curry or anything in that fancy restaurant, so I had some batata-puri and drank tea in Manmohan Shetty's office. Sure, I was broke and it was a hard struggle, but I was happy to be free.

Abhijat, if this book can manage to encourage even ten people who read it not to sell their soul and to keep striving towards their goal—the feeling they'll experience when they achieve what they hoped for will be something else— especially if they achieve it on their own terms. I believe I'm blessed to know that feeling.

AJ: You experienced that feeling when you were quite young. I mean it's rare for a young man in his early twenties to get an Oscar nomination. I bet the thought that *An Encounter with Faces* might get nominated never crossed your mind.

VVC: Arre, bilkul bhi nahin. [Not for a second.] It was beyond my wildest dreams. I did not even know my film had been submitted for the Oscars.

Nadeem Khan, the cameraman who shot *Murder at Monkey Hill*, called me to tell me about the nomination. My first reaction was: 'My friend, you're crazy. It must be India's entry. It doesn't mean the film has been nominated for an Oscar. That's a totally different ball game.'

Nadeem insisted he was right and said I should go and buy the newspaper and read it for myself. I rushed out and bought the *Times of India*. And there it was: 'Films Division named for Academy Award.'

I could see the words in print but I still thought it was impossible—there had to be some mistake. I called Films Division to confirm the news and they said the newspaper article was correct. That's when I said to myself: 'Shit! My film is nominated.'

AJ: You had no money, so how did you get to Los Angeles for the Oscars?

VVC: You're right, I didn't have the money to go to America. So I had to think of a solution. I took a train to Delhi to see Mr L.K. Advani in the hope that he could help me. I arrived in his office and was asked why I wanted to see him. I explained that my film was nominated for an Oscar and I had to go to the US urgently. They asked:

Do you have a passport?
No.
Visa?
No.
Ticket?
No.

They tried to get rid of me, but I insisted on meeting Mr Advani. I did not budge till I met him and explained the situation to him. As usual he was so helpful. He had a passport made for me within two hours, valid for six months, it was done without police verification. He gave me an economy-class ticket on Air India and $60 for three days' stay—$20 per day. All courtesy of the Government of India. It was very kind of him.

I had just enough money to buy a train ticket back to Bombay, but there was the problem of getting an American visa on time. The Oscar ceremony was on Monday, 9 April 1979, and I arrived in Bombay at 7 a.m. on the Saturday before. I rushed to the American Consulate in Breach Candy.

The first person I met at the Consulate was their watchman. I must have looked pretty rough as I hadn't slept all night on the train. The watchman took one look at me and spoke very rudely: 'You go, today's Saturday. Go!' I replied in Hindi: 'Why are you talking to me in English? Let me explain my problem to you.'

He shouted again in English and was even louder this time: 'You get out now! Or I'll call the police!'

I got furious and started shouting at him. Abhijat, you know my habit of using abusive language? Well, my old habit hasn't changed, though I have mellowed slightly over the years. [*both laugh*]

AJ: Yes, we're quite familiar with your way of speaking! Then what happened?

VVC: While I was shouting at the watchman, an American came out of the Consulate to find out what was going on. He looked at me and said:

> If you don't leave the premises, I'm afraid I'll have to call the police.

Sir, please listen to me. There's the Oscar ceremony in America this Monday.
What's that got to do with you?
Sir, my film has been nominated.
Your film? Nominated? Do you have any proof?

I showed him the newspaper cutting of Zanussi giving me the Golden Peacock Award and the *Times of India* piece confirming the nomination. I also showed him my shiny new passport and air ticket. I explained I had to have a visa that very day.

But it's Saturday. We're closed.
Sir, this is a very special thing for me. I'll miss the Oscars if I don't fly out tonight.

He stared at me for a few minutes, grabbed my passport and went inside. I had no idea if he'd give me a visa. He came out half an hour later and pointed to a page in my passport that was stamped with a one-week single-entry visa and said:

Next time, please don't make a scene here.
Sir, if I hadn't, I would not have got the visa.

We both laughed and I thanked him while he said: 'Looking at you, it's hard to imagine your film is nominated for an Oscar.'

I'll never forget him—he was a thin man and was wearing a white shirt. I owe him my trip to the Oscars. Once I had the visa, I rushed home, packed a small bag and got the Air India flight to Los Angeles that same night.

I landed in LA with hardly any money in my pocket. A friend told me I should look for motel business cards in the phone booths at the airport to find a place for the night. I dialled a few numbers, but hung up when I heard the voice on the other end. I thought I'd have better luck if I found a motel where an Indian worked. Finally I called the number of a motel called the La Cienega and immediately recognized an Indian accent saying 'hello'. I explained I was a film-maker from India, nominated for an Oscar but had no money and hoped he could help. His name was Mr Patel. He heard me out and promised to pick me up from the airport in his motel van. He arrived in no time at all.

I must tell you I was dying to have my first American meal but instead Mr Patel treated me to dinner at a restaurant called Devi and ordered a masala dosa for me with great affection.

AJ: Was that your first trip to America?

VVC: It was my first-ever trip abroad with my first-ever passport, thanks to Mr L.K. Advani. And my first dinner in the US was masala dosa, thanks to Mr Patel.

Next morning I had to buy a toothbrush because I had forgotten to pack one. I went in search of a shop. The first thing that struck me about Los Angeles was the smell of tyres. With all those cars driving around, the smell of rubber was everywhere. LA is not a city for walkers—everyone drives a car. I had to walk for what seemed miles before I found a shop. The shopkeeper was an Indian too and he helped me find what I needed.

So, the first two people I met in America were both Gujaratis. [*smiles*] When I returned to the motel, I called the Academy office and was told someone would come and pick me up that afternoon. A few hours later, a man knocked on my door. Still in my shorts, I opened the door and here was this stiff, formal gentleman in a tuxedo, saying: 'I'm here for Mr Vinod Chopra.' Of course he totally mispronounced my name.

Is this his room?
Yes, yes.
Young man, where's Mr Vinod Chopra?
I'm almost ready.
But where's Mr Chopra?
I am Vinod Chopra.
You're Vinod Chopra?

His face fell and his stiff demeanour vanished. He asked laughingly: 'How old are you, you f****r? You look like a sixteen-year-old and your film is nominated!'

He introduced himself as Michael London. I got dressed and he drove me to the Beverly Hilton where I was a guest of the Academy for two nights. Michael left me in this luxurious hotel room and I closed the door behind me. I had never seen such a fancy room. I jumped up and down on the spring bed. I looked into the marbled bathroom with its shiny mirrors and stared out of the wide window on to Beverly Hills.

Man! I was in Hollywood! This boy from a small mohalla in Kashmir had landed in the heart of movieland! When I calmed myself down, I decided to ring my sister Shelly who was living in Canada in Moose Jaw.

AJ: All this happened on the Sunday?

VVC: Yes, the day before the Oscars. I made a collect call to Shelly and told her I was in LA at the Beverly Hilton. She said in a jokey voice:

> Tell me where you're really calling from.
> *Shelly, I'm really at the Beverly Hilton. My film is nominated for an Oscar.*
> So when are you meeting President Carter?
> *I'm serious, Shelly.*
> If you're serious, tell me where you are.
> *At the Beverly Hilton.*
> Seriously? Then give me your room number. I'll call you back.

I gave her my room number and she hung up. A minute later the phone rang and when I said 'hello', there was dead silence. Then I heard Shelly say excitedly: 'Haye, Vidhu Praji! Tussi Oscar-nominated? [Vidhu, my brother, you've been nominated for an Oscar!] You're staying at the Beverly Hilton?' I mumbled 'yes'. She was in complete shock.

The dress code for the Oscar ceremony was either a black tie and tuxedo or one's national dress. I didn't have the money to hire a tux, so I wore what I usually wear to sleep at night—a khadi kurta-pyjama and it passed off as my national dress. [*smiles*]

A car came to pick me up next day and we headed to the Dorothy Chandler Pavilion for the fifty-first Oscar ceremony. Just before the start of the ceremony, we were told not to move from our seats because we were on camera. This woman who was sitting next to me kept getting up, so I reminded her we were not supposed to move about. She apologized. Then they announced the Oscar for Best Actress and we heard the famous words . . . and the Oscar goes to . . . Jane Fonda.

This lady who was sitting next to me gets up and goes onto the stage to receive her award for *Coming Home*. It was Jane Fonda! [*laughs*] I was so embarrassed. In my excitement, I had not recognized her. She came back and I apologized profusely: 'I'm so sorry, I didn't know you were Jane Fonda.' She gave me a lovely smile and said even if I had known who she was, I was right to tell her to stay seated.

After the ceremony, we went to the Governors Ball for dinner. By then I was pretty pissed off because I hadn't won. You know I was young and naïve and so sure I'd win that I had foolishly even written an acceptance speech that I kept in my pocket. When I didn't win I thought to myself: 'Hey! What happened here?'

Directors Jacqueline Phillips Shedd and Ben Shedd won the Oscar that year for their short, *The Flight of the Gossamer Condor.* At the Governors Ball, Ben came up to me and said how much he loved *An Encounter* . . . He asked how much raw stock I had exposed. I said:

Four thousand feet.

No, no, I know your final film is 2200 ft but what was your shooting ratio?

I'm not sure you'll believe me but I only had 4000 ft of 35 mm black-and-white stock.

Impossible! So how did you do it?

I turned on the camera when the kids who were talking said something I could use. It was like editing in camera, that's how.

Ben nearly passed out. I asked him how much raw stock he had exposed and he said 150,000 ft. I was dumbstruck and all I could say was: 'Congratulations!'

AJ: You also met Francis Ford Coppola that night at the Governors Ball.

VVC: Yes. My producer from Films Division, K.K. Kapil, was very happy and very high. I was standing about five feet away from Coppola, who was talking to Michael Cimino, the winner of the Best Director Award that year for *Deer Hunter*. Kapil asked me who I was staring at and I said: 'Francis Ford Coppola. He made *The Godfather*.'

I told Kapil I had come five thousand miles hoping to meet Francis Ford Coppola, but now lacked the guts to take five steps towards him. Before I could stop Kapil, he walked over to Coppola, tapped him on the shoulder and said: 'Hello, hello, excuse me. My director's film has been nominated for an Oscar. He wants to meet you.'

I felt so embarrassed. I had two options; I could either make a run for it or walk up to Coppola. I finally plucked up the courage and when I was near him, I said:

I'm sorry, I'm the one responsible for the intrusion into your privacy. My producer is happy and drunk, he doesn't know who you are.
Are you nominated?
For a short film.
Welcome. Now you're here, stay and make good movies.
I've got to go back to India.
No, you should stay.
If the Godfather wishes . . .

He laughed and invited me to San Francisco to visit his Zoetrope Studio. How could I miss such a chance? So I went there a few days later. I was very impressed with his sprawling studio—there was an avenue named after Akira Kurosawa, a Federico Fellini Lane and a Sergei Eisenstein Park. Coppola's guys asked me if I wanted to stay longer, but I was madly in love with Renu; we had only recently got married and I couldn't stay away from home.

The visit to Zoetrope really moved me. Of course, I was very keen to work with Coppola and his team. Years later, in 1982, I wrote a screenplay called *Sasha: The Lost Prince* and sent it to them. Coppola's studio sent back a letter signed by Fred Roos, who happened to work as an executive producer for a while on my film *Broken Horses* in 2014—one of life's interesting coincidences. Roos's letter said they liked the script and would keep it on the backburner. I didn't really understand what the 'backburner' meant. I still have their letter somewhere.

AJ: You were very confident to send a script to Coppola!

VVC: I always had the 'Munna Bhai' confidence! But at that time I looked physically very young. So when I was about to post my script to Coppola, we decided to send my photograph along with it. I combed my hair back, wore phoney specs, all in the hope of coming across older than I looked. I had to show them I was someone with the authority and confidence of a director. [*both laugh*]

AJ: What did you take away from the Oscar experience?

VVC: It made me feel someday I should be making that acceptance speech. I was that naïve.

You create mountains to climb and when you manage to climb the first mountain, you create an even higher one. I think that's what I've done all my life. You never know if you're good enough unless you try.

AJ: When the excitement of the Oscars was over, did you fly straight back to Bombay?

VVC: No, no. Shelly sent me a ticket from LA to Moose Jaw. We hadn't met for some years and were keen to spend a few days together—I had never visited Canada or seen Shelly in her own home. I didn't know if I'd ever get the chance to travel outside of India again. This trip was a minor miracle in itself!

Before I left Bombay, I had bought myself a really cheap pair of shoes to wear at the Oscars. I did not realize the outsoles on the shoes were red. When Shelly and I went for a walk, unknown to me, my shoes left a trail of red on the beautiful white snow. Some passers-by stopped and stared at us since those red stains looked like drops of blood. It was embarrassing as hell!

Soon enough I had to return home. Because I had changed my original booking, I ended up flying from Moose Jaw to Toronto, Toronto to London, London to Moscow, Moscow to Delhi and then Delhi to Bombay. That was the cheapest way home.

AJ: Didn't Naseeruddin Shah give you a lift from Delhi to Bombay on this trip?

VVC: No, that was an earlier trip. I had completely forgotten about that.

Naseer was my batch mate at the FTII, and he had just bought a Fiat in Delhi because it was cheaper there, so we drove it all the way to Bombay. I did something very cheeky. Naseer and I didn't have enough money to stay in a half-decent place on the way, so I suggested we go to a government guest house. I told the caretaker about how my film had been nominated for an Oscar and that the Government of India had given me a ticket to America, etc. He was duly impressed. We gave him ten rupees and he let us spend the night there.

That reminds me—when Naseer visited America for the first time, he bought a lapel pin for me there, I think it was from the Dollar Store, that read, 'I refuse to grow up.' He gifted it to me in jest. When I went to his fiftieth birthday party, almost three decades later, I wore that lapel pin on my shirt. Naseer couldn't believe I had kept it for all these years. I told him: 'See? I still follow your advice!' We had tears in our eyes and hugged each other like brothers. That pin is in my study somewhere.

AJ: It's been a long journey, starting from your early fascination for Hollywood and foreign cinema to making your own movies.

If I remember correctly, one of the first films that fascinated you was the 1958 British thriller *Chase a Crooked Shadow*. I don't think you saw the film in Kashmir but someone told you the story.

VVC: That's right. I hadn't seen the film. When my elder brother, Ravi Praji, visited us in Srinagar from Bombay where he was living, he told my father about the film. Then my father recounted the story to me sometime later.

There I was living with my extended family at 35A Wazir Bagh in this little mohalla, discovering the big wide world through cinema. We were so young, and perhaps the idea of going to America someday and making a movie there was planted in my mind when I heard the story of *Chase a Crooked Shadow*. Who knows!

I can still hear my father's voice describing the last scene of the film where the heroine tells a man who, she believes, is pretending to be her brother: 'How can you be my brother? I killed him with my own hands.' The man then picks up the phone and says: 'This is the inspector. She has confessed to her crime.' The inspector puts the phone down. Fade out. The end.

It was my father sitting in our small dimly lit room in Kashmir recounting the story, scene by scene, that stayed with me ever since. When I saw the actual film years later, it didn't make as great an impression as my father's version. [*laughs*] I suppose that's how memory works.

For many years I thought *Chase a Crooked Shadow* was directed by Alfred Hitchcock, then I learnt Michael Anderson had directed it. I'm eternally grateful to him for making the film. It changed my life.

AJ: It's not surprising you thought it was Hitchcock because it looks like a Hitchcock film. The lighting, the atmosphere—it's a great film.

By the way, what language did you speak at home? Was it Kashmiri?

VVC: My mother and father could speak Kashmiri, but we spoke Punjabi at home. Our family was originally from the Punjab, though we settled in Kashmir many generations earlier. I can speak Punjabi but I can't write it.

AJ: Where in the Punjab did your parents come from?

VVC: They were originally from Peshawar. My father, Lala Dinanath Chopra, led a very modest life, but an interesting one. He was married at the age of fifteen and fathered a son, Ramanand Chopra, who later became famous as Ramanand Sagar. Then came the second son whom they named Chitranjan.

In 1927, my father's first wife died; and several years later, he remarried. My mother's name was Shanti Devi, though my father called her Subhag Rani. She had six sisters.

At the time when my parents were getting married, my father was working as a post office cashier. He was not particularly well-to-do, but was known for his honesty, so he was approached by the regional head of the Birla Group and offered the job as the branch secretary of their Ruby General Insurance Company—it was not a fully-fledged branch at that time. The job came with the option of my father becoming an insurance agent, which they said would add substantially to his income. But he was exceptionally sensitive when it came to his sense of self-respect, so he refused by saying he was happy just being the branch secretary. Sometime later, the company, in appreciation of his unfailing honesty, made him the branch manager of their new Srinagar branch.

By the time I was born, on 5 September 1952, my father had been promoted to district manager, since Ruby General Insurance had opened a second office in Jammu. He was moderately educated; I believe he had studied till the tenth standard. Despite his lack of a formal education, my father knew how to manage reasonably well in English. He was well respected by everyone in the community and was invited to become a member of Srinagar's Rotary Club.

I have always shared this belief with my father that a home is very important. I remember loving our Wazir Bagh house and its front lawn. I used to spend hours there, lying on the grass in the winter—in the 'sardi ki dhoop' [the wintry sun]. Javed Sahib has used that image in the song 'Ek ladki ko dekha . . .'

So many years have passed but I still have dreams of being in that house. I'm always back in Kashmir in my dreams.

AJ: How many of you lived in the Wazir Bagh house?

VVC: My father had seven sons, including Ramanand Sagar and Chitranjan, from his first marriage. But they left home before I was born and by the early 1950s, Ramanand Sagar had made a name for himself in films, writing screenplays for very big hits like Raj Kapoor's *Barsaat*.

The funny thing is, until I went to film school, I had no idea they were my half-brothers. I assumed they were my real brothers. Nobody talked about it. My mother had a young face, so I did wonder how she could have such grown-up sons. When I asked her, she told me she had married very young, but did not say they were not her sons.

AJ: You have only one sister?

VVC: Yes, my younger sister, Shelly.

You may not know this, but I was an unwanted child because I was the seventh boy in the family, and my mother had really wanted a daughter. She had a close friend, a Mrs

Darshana Kapoor, who didn't have any children, so she told Mrs Kapoor that if she gave birth to another son, she'd give Mrs Kapoor the baby. But my father scuttled the idea.

Today I could have been Vinod Kapoor instead of Vinod Chopra. [*both laugh*]

AJ: Was your father a disciplinarian?

VVC: He was very strict about his value system. We were shit-scared of him if ever he lost his temper. Did I tell you that I used to steal when I was young? I started stealing from the age of eight and this went on till I was fifteen. I used the money to buy things that I enjoyed eating.

In our family, we had a tradition of sitting together at mealtimes. A couple of times a week, we would have lamb or paneer. My mother served everyone and we all got our fair share—typically two small pieces of lamb or paneer. We were given a fixed amount of food on a thali. And that's all we would have. No second helpings. Even after all these years, I still think it's fascinating I can now have as many helpings as I want, because that's not how we were brought up.

AJ: So you stole to buy things to eat. Who did you steal from?

VVC: From the gods. When my mother prayed in our puja room, she put a few coins in a small tin of Lipton tea that she sealed with dhoop. Tea was sold in square tin boxes back then, so this was her kind of piggy bank. So with a thin bit of wire, I had mastered the art of prising a few coins out of the box. I became quite skilled at it. I was studying at DAV School in Amira Kadal, and during the lunch break I would buy sweets and chhole-bhature from the tuck shop with the money I stole.

I did not take all the coins from her tin box in one go, so my mother didn't realize for a long time what I was doing. But then I became greedy and overconfident and one day I took out all the coins and left only one coin in the tin box. That made everyone suspicious.

The next day my mother and my elder brother, Vijay Praji, hid in the adjoining room and through a hole in the wooden slats watched me fiddling with the wire and the piggy bank. As soon as I prised out a coin, they came into the room and caught me red-handed. My mother slapped the hell out of me.

AJ: Did you steal from anyone else in the family?

VVC: Yes, from my brother Vir. He has always been a diligent person, and even when he was young, he would save money. Vir got his PhD from the London School of Economics. So you know the kind of young man he was.

One day my grandmother, whom we called 'Beji', saw me stealing Vir's money. She asked me what I was doing. I was often offhand with her and said almost rudely: 'Mere paise hain, tussi ki dekh rahe ho.' [It's my money! Why are you bothered?]

With Vir's money I bought gol gappas from a Bengali who sold snacks in our mohalla. In the meantime, Beji, who was mad at me, told Vir what I had done. He followed me to the stall, and as I was about to put the first gol gappa in my mouth, I felt his hand grip mine. He asked me sternly:

How much did you steal?
Eight annas.

He forced me to put the gol gappa down and would not let me finish it. When we got home, he said nothing to the others and I thought: 'That's great, the incident will stay between us brothers.'

The next morning when my father came home from the temple—he would visit the temple every day—he announced: 'The primary classes have a holiday today. Only Vir will go to school.'

The idea of not going to school obviously made me very happy and I started playing in the garden when I saw our house help, Joginder Singh, picking some 'saddar booti' leaves—it's a kind of poison ivy. I got very worried and asked him why he needed them. He said he was making a medicinal mix. So I carried on playing without a care in the world.

An hour or so later my father called me to his room. I was not sure why he wanted me there. He shut the door behind me and said: 'I'm going to teach you a lesson today. You're never going to steal again.'

He made me take off my clothes, stand naked and hit me hard with the poison ivy leaves. You can imagine what happened. My body was on fire, my mother was screaming outside the door—all hell broke loose. I was in great pain but I was a very headstrong little brat and in between the blows, I told him in Punjabi: 'Jab tussi buddhe ho jaaoge, main tenu maranga.' [When you get older, it'll be my turn to hit you.]

In the middle of the whipping and the screaming, my father asked what I had done with the money. I was in agony but my insolence was still intact. I said: 'I buy snacks I like eating. Things that you can't give me at home.'

When he heard me say that, he beat me even harder. Finally my mother rescued me and took me into another room and made me lie down on a fatta [wooden plank]. She covered me with a mud paste to cool my body down. My skin was burning and itchy. I was in sheer hell for days.

AJ: That must have put an end to your stealing.

VVC: For sure it did! [*both laugh*]

Abhijat, you're taking me on a journey that feels like we're visiting another planet, meeting some other Vidhu Vinod Chopra.

AJ: I am sure it feels like that! But tell me, why did your father punish you so severely?

VVC: He was a very honest man and the idea that his son could steal was intolerable to him.

I recall another incident. Shakti Sweets is an institution in Srinagar. It's a huge shop on Residency Road that sells every kind of Indian mithai. All the guys from S.P. College used to go there. One day a friend of mine decided to treat me to a gulab jamun so we went to Shakti Sweets. The gulab jamun was served in a bowl with a spoon. As we did not have any spoons at home, I thought: 'Why not pocket the spoon?'

We had our gulab jamun and I headed home. That night when everyone was eating daal, I took out the spoon to scoop up the daal. I wanted to show off. My father saw the spoon and asked where it came from. I said cheekily:

Shakti Sweets.
How much did you pay for it?
I didn't buy it.
So?
They served gulab jamun with the spoon.
And you stole it?

My father heard me out and then made me go to the sweet-maker's house and return the spoon. There was no waiting till the morning as far as my father was concerned. It was after nine at night and it was very cold. He sent our house help Joginder Singh with me to make sure I returned the spoon. So, we walked to the owner's house in the cold and dark.

I could feel tears rolling down my face. I felt humiliated. I knocked at the gate. Silence. I knocked harder. No one came. Some minutes passed and still there was no sign of anyone. The gates of most houses in Kashmir were some distance from the main house, so the owner of Shakti Sweets had to make his way from his house, cross a huge courtyard, walk across the lawn and open the gate. By the time he got to the gate, I could see he was absolutely furious. I quickly said:

Spoon.
What spoon?
I took it by mistake.

I thought he'd show me some gratitude seeing me shivering in the cold, but instead he shouted loudly at me: 'Why the hell couldn't you wait till the morning to bring it back? You should've come to my shop in the morning and not to my home at this ungodly hour.'

Before he could wake up all the neighbours with his shouting, Joginder Singh and I quickly slipped away. That was my father, sending me there so late at night. Honesty meant everything to him.

AJ: Do you think you're more like him or your mother in temperament?

VVC: I'm more like my father. I am a happy man like he was, but if someone behaves in a dishonest way, I can blow a fuse very easily. Then they can expect a flood of MC/BC abuse! As you know, I am known for swearing when I lose my temper. I've calmed down thanks to Anupama. Our married life has calmed me down. But I can get very angry just like my father used to. My mother was a gentle soul. Vir takes after her.

AJ: Vir is the brother who looked after you, right?

VVC: Yes, all my life.

AJ: Tell me more about your mother.

VVC: She fasted every year on Karva Chauth. You know the tradition—married women fast for the health of their husbands from sunrise till the moon is out. So before dawn, we children gathered in our tiny kitchen and she fed us barfi and seviyaan. We were a lower-middle-class family, so this was a big treat. There's another thing I remember— she would put some Nivea cream on her palm, not too much because it was expensive, and ragdo [rub rigorously] the cream on my face to soften my skin.

Another memory that has stayed with me for sixty-odd years—we were living in Jammu at the time and my mom, Vir and I shared a bed. So when we slept at night, my mother's head faced in one direction and mine was in the opposite direction. One night when I was half-asleep and feeling cold, I felt her hand pull my pyjama leg down. It had probably rolled up because I was tossing and turning in my sleep. She covered me with a quilt and it made me feel so warm and protected. That memory has never left me.

AJ: I'd like to talk about your school. You said you went to DAV High School.

VVC: It was a less expensive Hindi-medium school, while the rich boys in Srinagar went to English-medium schools like Burn Hall School or Biscoe. Sometimes I would watch the boys from the other schools; they spoke English and played cricket.

My school fees was two rupees a month. Everybody spoke Hindi and Urdu at DAV, but we wrote in Devanagari. I couldn't write Urdu beyond the alphabet. Most people spoke Kashmiri, though it was not taught at our school.

We had a class called 'Dharam Shiksha', where we chanted prayers in Sanskrit. We had Arya Samaj havans every alternate Sunday. I was pretty clever and most of the time, I topped the class.

AJ: Who were your school friends?

VVC: Let's put it this way—I didn't really have friends. I was not the 'friend' type. I was the class monitor and used to bash everyone up. Nobody was my friend and I was nobody's friend. Jia Lal Khanna, a rich merchant's son, was the closest person I had for a friend. Frankly, even when I was at the film institute, I didn't have close friends. Ashok Ahuja and I were roommates and we got on very well while we were there.

If you ask me how many friends I have now, I'd have to say I don't really have friends. I have my family and my cinema-family like you, Abhijat. And there's Raju, Anuja, Yogesh, Jassi, Shikhar, Abhishek, Ramakant . . . I can't name everybody here, it's a long list. But I love you all as much as I love my biological family.

I don't think people understand the meaning of friendship. I think they mistake acquaintances for friends. A friend is a very big thing. What is a friend? A friend is like a brother or a sister—someone for whom you'd do anything. I believe friends must be like-minded. Like Anu is my friend because we're like-minded and it's not only because we're married to each other.

AJ: When you're troubled, who do you talk to?

VVC: Mostly to Anu. But I'm not a guy who takes trouble home.

Why does a computer slow down? Because there are too many programmes running at the same time. How to remedy the situation? You press the delete button and get rid of as many programmes as you can. You can say I have a very efficient delete button. Even when I read a text message from some idiot, I block the number and delete the SMS, so I never have to look at it again.

My life is uncluttered. Let me show you my cell phone— let's take today—there's a call from my architect. Then, Abhijat, you called and I tried calling A.R. Rahman on Facetime. So three calls today.

AJ: But we don't know how many your assistant Anuja has received!

VVC: Yeah, her life is cluttered. [*both laugh*]

AJ: How do you spend your day?

VVC: I wake up early in the morning and the first thing I do is thank the Lord. Then I practise shavasana and ask myself, what if I were to die now? Would I die a happy man? On most days the answer is yes, so I go back to sleep. Some days the answer is no, that's when I sit up and think how I can go about fixing things.

It's said that some Sufi saints in Kashmir sleep in coffins. When they wake up in the morning and step out of the coffin, they thank the Lord for the blessing of another day. That tells you how temporary life is. We're not here forever, so we need to be at peace with oneself.

I believe the way to be at peace really depends on your deeds account, if I may call it that—that account should not have a negative balance.

AJ: You're so right. [*pause*]

Coming back to the old days and how you started to love cinema. I remember there was another Hollywood film that made an impact on you—the 1966 American movie *Gambit*. I remember you saying you did not know the meaning of the title and your brother Vir-ji said it meant 'Dhoka' [deceit].

VVC: Yeah, that's what he said.

Gambit was a huge influence on me. There was a cinema in Srinagar called the Broadway and they had started showing English-language films at 7 p.m. The showtimes for the Hindi films were at 1 p.m., 4 p.m. and 9 p.m. The Bond films and action movies usually played at the Broadway because the owner, a gentleman called Vijay Dhar, loved cinema.

Besides *Gambit*, another movie made a great impression on me—it was a 1964 black-and-white thriller called

Strait-Jacket. It's a story about a mother and daughter. The mother, played by Joan Crawford, is called Lucy. Diane Baker is her daughter, Carol. In the first scene, we see a woman killing a man brutally with an axe. Lucy is arrested for murder and sent to a mental asylum.

Many years later, when she is released, people are found murdered again. All fingers point to Lucy, but her daughter keeps providing an alibi for her mother. In the final scene, we see a woman wielding an axe and Lucy walks in demanding that the attacker reveal her identity. Lucy pulls off the axe-killer's wig and it's none other than her daughter Carol who has been impersonating her mother and butchering people.

Strait-Jacket has an amazing storyline. When I saw the film, there were very few people in the cinema, because it didn't have a big star cast. I saw it at the Palladium Cinema, which was showing English-language films by then. Unlike the Broadway, the Palladium screened mainly B-grade movies and horror movies.

After I saw *Strait-Jacket*, I was too scared to sleep alone in my room. I kept imagining a woman coming at me with an axe. Then one night I suddenly woke up, looked at the door and shouted out loud: 'Okay, come and kill me, I'm not scared. Come on, kill me now!' Of course no one came. I still remember that night clearly. Don't forget I was only twelve. After that I was no longer scared at night.

AJ: You were a teenager in the 1960s and that was the time colour was introduced in a big way in Hindi films. As a result, the beautiful scenery of Kashmir became a favourite location, especially when it came to picturizing songs. You must have seen films like *Junglee* or *Kashmir Ki Kali*, what did you make of them? Did Kashmiris like these films?

VVC: Cinema was a big deal in Kashmir. Films had good audiences. What else was there for us as far as entertainment was concerned? There was no TV, nothing. So Hindi film stars were like gods to us.

Oh yes, I was fascinated. I would've given my right arm to be Shammi Kapoor sitting in a shikara on the Dal Lake surrounded by all those beauties rowing their boats and singing 'Tareef karoon kya uski'. Wow! When I directed Shammi Kapoor in *Kareeb*, I told him how much he meant to us.

Did you know Ramanand Sagar's 1965 film *Arzoo* was filmed in Kashmir and Rajendra Kumar and Sadhana came to Srinagar for the shoot? They were stars and did not feel human to me. When Ramanand Sagar brought Sadhana home to 35A Wazir Bagh for Diwali, I couldn't utter a single word. I just kept staring at her. It was Diwali and firecrackers were being lit. Sadhana accidentally kicked a firecracker that landed on my hand. My hand was burnt and I screamed. She came rushing over, held my hand and applied some cream on it. When I went to school the next day, I told everybody: 'Sadhana came to our home for Diwali. She burnt my hand. Look!'

I proudly showed them my wound. I didn't want it to heal quickly. I treated my burn mark like a badge of honour.

To me Sadhana's presence felt like an angel had descended. The *Arzoo* cast and crew stayed at the very expensive Oberoi Palace Hotel in Srinagar which later became the Lalit Grand Palace. We used to look at the hotel from afar and say: 'Oh, that's where rich people stay.' It was unimaginable to me that one day I'd be staying in the same hotel as those stars and even filming there. Life has been kind to me.

AJ: What was the first Hindi film you ever saw?

VVC: I don't remember, but V. Shantaram's *Navrang* was the first film that took me by surprise. It starts in black and white, but at the very beginning of the film, there's a shot of nine ghadas [large pots] and as colour pours out of them, the image turns from black and white to colour. Oh my God! That was a big moment. Much later, I even told V. Shantaram when I met him at his mixing studio during the making of *Khamosh* how fascinated I was with that shot. He was such a genius.

But no one mattered to me more than Dilip Kumar. When I was growing up, he was the number one guy for me. When he dies at the end of *Ganga Jumna*—I could not believe he could ever die. I used to go around the house pretending I was Dilip Kumar. I walked like him, talked like him. And in my mind I was him! It drove my mother crazy. When I came home after watching *Gopi*, I could not stop imitating the way the Gopi character speaks. My mother got so fed up, she would scream at me, saying: 'Stop it now!'

I do not even remember how many times I saw *Ram Aur Shyam*. I couldn't afford the ticket, so I sat in the cinema lobby with my ears pressed to the big entrance door so I could hear bits of dialogue seeping through. I knew every line by heart.

When Ram gets bashed up and is asked if he is scared of Gajendra Babu (played by Pran), he raises his hand to his mouth and, covering it with the sleeve of his kurta, speaks in a terrified tone. [*VVC imitates the action and whispers the lines*]

AJ: Wow! That's a perfect imitation of Dilip Kumar. You even have his voice down to a T. [*both laugh*]

VVC: Can you believe it? You see I was obsessed with the guy. All I wanted was to be like him. I didn't want to be Shammi Kapoor or Raj Kapoor, I wanted to be Dilip Kumar.

AJ: Tell me what happened when you met him.

VVC: It was just amazing. Actually he came a few times to our house in Pali Hill. He even autographed the poster of *Mughal-e-Azam* that's in my study. When he saw *3 Idiots*, he raved about the film. We had a long chat about the directors he worked with in the past.

I asked him about Mehboob Khan and K. Asif. He praised Mehboob Khan and said what a gentleman he was. But he had nothing good to say about K. Asif and thought he was a rough man who shouted too much. He added:

Thank God I never worked with him.
Sir, what are you saying? You made Mughal-e-Azam *with K. Asif!*
Oh no! I forgot!

And we both laughed.

AJ: When we look at your early films like *Sazaye Maut*, *Khamosh* and even *Parinda*, we can see the fascination you had for the crime thriller. But your fascination with that form was not restricted to Hollywood movies because you were also an avid reader of crime novels. Am I remembering correctly?

VVC: Yes. I must tell you I learnt how to speak English when I was about sixteen. In the fifth or sixth standard, they taught us the English alphabet, in eighth standard it was 'Ram is coming, Shyam is going . . .' It was only during college, when I was seventeen, that I could finally read English and that's when I started reading James Hadley Chase. Till that point in time I was engrossed in books like *Jasoosi Duniya* by Ibn-e-Safi BA. For some reason, Ibn-e-Safi added 'BA' to his name. I found that intriguing.

When we were kids, we ran a little book club that had about a hundred Hindi books donated by us readers. We organized the books by numbers—so there was a Vinod Chopra book number twenty, and a friend in the group would say: 'Achha, main eight number ki kitaab tujhe de raha hoon. [Okay, I'm lending you book number eight.] In exchange, I'll borrow book number twenty.'

We were all great fans of Ibn-e-Safi's detective series, *Jasoosi Duniya*. Every month a new novel came out and sometimes they had special issues. We waited anxiously for his new books, and if we knew it would be in the shops, say, on the fifteenth of August, we queued up from the fourteenth. We had very little money between us, so the guy who paid for the book had the right to read it first, then it got passed on to the others.

In the Hindi version, Ibn-e-Safi's heroes were called Colonel Vinod and Captain Hameed. Vinod had a different name in the original Urdu and was Colonel Faridi. And there was a comical fat guy called Qasim. I don't know why Vinod was called 'colonel' because he was not an army officer, but an inspector. And why Hameed was called 'captain' when he was a sergeant. Anyway, Colonel Vinod and Captain Hameed solved cases like Sherlock Holmes and Dr Watson. We were fascinated by them.

Ibn-e-Safi created great names for his characters, and Abhijat, I must say, Raju and you also work very hard on the names of your characters. Think of 'Ranchoddas Shamaldas Chanchad' or 'Phunsukh Wangdu'.

I personally think names are very important. They tell a story in themselves and sometimes even give us clues about the temperament of the characters.

AJ: You're so right about that.

I remember you were a great fan of Ibn-e-Safi and when his books were reprinted recently, you immediately ordered copies.

VVC: I tried to read them again and couldn't.

AJ: But I did. It was important for me to understand what you were reading when you were growing up. His books are quite good.

Talking of Ibn-e-Safi reminds me of the time we were in the car with your wife Anu, and she and I were discussing Shakespeare's sonnets and she started reciting a poem. You went silent for a long time and then suddenly said: 'Aur phir Colonel Vinod ne peechhe se goli chalaayi.' [Then Colonel Vinod fired a bullet.]

We were taken aback and you added: 'Don't give me a complex about not reading Shakespeare. Hum ne yehi padha hai, toh hum yehi recite karenge.' [This is what I used to read and this is what I'll recite.]

VVC: [*laughs*] I remember that car journey!

The other book I liked very much is the conversation between Alfred Hitchcock and François Truffaut. Akira Kurosawa's *Something Like an Autobiography* is really inspiring too. I liked the books of Simone de Beauvoir and Jean-Paul Sartre. Renu used to say she was Simone de Beauvoir and I was Jean-Paul Sartre.

I learnt a lot from books—maybe one day someone might read this book when I'm dead and gone and say: 'A man from a small mohalla in Kashmir can have big dreams and fulfil them without selling his soul, so why can't I?'

AJ: And they might also discover how hard you worked to achieve those dreams.

I didn't know you in those days but I must tell you when I was growing up, seeing *Khamosh* was a special experience for me. It had Shabana Azmi, Amol Palekar and Naseeruddin Shah and it was the first truly polished and sophisticated Hindi film thriller I had seen. It ran for a little over ninety minutes and had me gripped. And this was at a time when Hindi films dragged on and on for almost three hours.

Khamosh reminded me of *Chase a Crooked Shadow*, Hitchcock's films, Ibn-e-Safi and James Hadley Chase— all rolled into one!

VVC: [*smiles*] I'm glad you liked it. The film got good reviews when it was released. I know that Anil Kapoor agreed to work with me in *Parinda* because he had seen *Khamosh*.

The film was made on a shoestring budget of about eight lakhs. I don't know how we did it. I remember wanting to have the first screening in Kashmir because Mr Narinder Singh, the owner of Pahalgam Hotel, helped me make it. He let me film in his hotel for free and I was very grateful to him. For many reasons I felt it was right to go back to my roots and show the film at Broadway. It took me back to the years when I sat in that hall mesmerized by the movies I was devouring. When the film started, everyone went quiet. Ten minutes into the story, two guys behind me said in Kashmiri: 'Oh my God, this is a f***g Hollywood movie!'

I was thrilled to hear those words. When I returned to Bombay, I arranged a show of *Khamosh* at the preview theatre Dimple and invited many top producers and distributors. Yash Chopra came and Rajiv Rai. After the film was over, I saw Yash Chopra waiting for me outside the preview theatre. It was raining, but he waited till I came out so he could compliment me. He said he loved the film. I was so happy I told Renu: 'Wow, we've done it!' You can imagine how happy we were.

When I look back, I'm talking about the mid-1980s, it's only now I think: 'Oh my God, we were so poor.' At that time, Renu and I did not think of ourselves as poor or victims of any kind. But we were poor! I remember we had to think twice about going out to eat. When we could afford it, we'd go to one of two local restaurants—they both happened to be called Neelam. The Neelam closer to us, we were living in Pali Naka then, was in Khar, and the other Neelam was next to the Bandra railway station. I remember rajma-chawal cost about a rupee and 25 paise for a plate at the Khar Neelam and 50 paise at the Bandra railway station one. We used to walk the extra mile to the station to save 75 paise. But the day *Khamosh* was praised, we went to Neelam, the expensive one, and had a hearty meal.

The humourist P.L. Deshpande once said: 'We were poor, but we were so happy that we didn't have time to feel our poverty.' Our life mirrored his words.

The morning after the screening at Dimple, we received a bouquet of beautiful flowers with a card from Gulshan Rai and Rajiv Rai saying: 'Congratulations.' We were barely able to make ends meet, and there we were holding this beautiful bunch of flowers. We rushed out and bought a bottle of Old Monk Rum and Coke to celebrate this big event in our lives. Since Gulshan Rai was the biggest producer and distributor at that time, we were sure *Khamosh* would get released.

The situation then was no different from me telling a young film-maker today that his film is brilliant. He'd be over the moon, but also assume I might help him in some significant way.

For the next few days, Renu and I and the telephone never parted. We did not step out of the house together, in case Gulshan Rai rang. If I went out to buy vegetables, Renu stayed by the phone, in case Gulshan Rai rang. And if she had to go out on an errand, I stayed by the phone, in case Gulshan Rai rang.

Days passed and there was no call. So, we decided to go and see Gulshan Rai. I knew his offices were in a building called Everest in Tardeo. His staff made us wait outside his room for half an hour and finally Gulshan Rai called us in. He had a massive office that seemed like a stadium to us. He spoke in Punjabi:

Haan-ji? Yes?
I made the film Khamosh.
Good film. Yes?
You saw the film and sent us flowers?
I sent you flowers? I didn't send you flowers.

He picked up the phone and asked his son Rajiv if he had sent flowers to us. His son said yes. So he dispatched us to his son's office, which was smaller than his father's room. Rajiv Rai spoke with a slight American accent and was very nice:

I saw your film. What a movie! Well done!
Will you buy it and distribute it?

My father does the distribution. I'm just telling you what I think, as one film-maker to another.

I just lost it and blurted out a whole lot of abuse that I don't want to repeat here: 'You praise my film but you won't help to distribute it?' I was beside myself and finally Renu stopped me and dragged me out of there. When I came out of their offices, I was still furious.

I am sure the reason why, years later, I became a producer was in a way to help the young man I once was. When Raju narrated the script of *Munna Bhai* to me, I felt as if a young Vinod was looking for a producer. Most of the films I've produced were made by first-time directors because I know how it feels when no one believes in you and there's no helping hand.

AJ: Is that why you have helped so many people to join films?

VVC: Actually, I had no idea I had helped so many first-timers till Sony Television came to me wanting me to be the main judge on a show called *The X Factor*. At that time I had no interest in being a judge on a reality TV show. But I didn't know how to say no to them, so I quoted an astronomical figure as a fee—an offer they would've had to refuse! But to my astonishment, the Sony team came over to discuss the details of the engagement. So I asked them: 'Guys, why are you paying me so much? Why do you think I am worth such a high fee? This is too much!'

They explained the reason was because they knew many people had thanked me at various film awards for giving them an early break in their careers. I was surprised, but then they put a list of names on the table before me. When I looked at the list I could see that, yes, Vidya Balan started with me, so had Boman Irani. Nana Patekar's big break came in *Parinda*; Sanjay Leela Bhansali was my assistant on *Parinda* and *1942: A Love Story*; Sudhir Mishra assisted me in *Khamosh*; and of course there's Raju Hirani who edited *Mission Kashmir* for me. Not forgetting even you, dear Abhijat Joshi, you started with me.

There's also Shantanu Moitra who composed the music for *Parineeta* and Swanand Kirkire who wrote the lyrics. *Mission Kashmir* gave Shankar–Ehsaan–Loy their first major break. Even Hrithik Roshan's first major film outside of his father's films was *Mission Kashmir*. In terms of movies by first-time directors, there was Raju Hirani's *Munna Bhai M.B.B.S.*, Rajesh Mapuskar's *Ferrari Ki Sawaari,* Pradeep Sarkar's *Parineeta*. Bejoy Nambiar made *Wazir*, his first big production, with me. We also made a mainstream LGBTQ film, *Ek Ladki Ko Dekha Toh Aisa Laga*, with first-time director Shelly, who you know is my sister. Nitin Desai started his career with me in *1942: A Love Story* and today he owns a studio. There were more people on that list, but I can't recall them all now.

I like working with first-timers. If we don't help young talent, particularly people who are not members of a film family, who will? When it came to *Shikara*, as you know, we cast new actors, Aadil and Sadia, and many other newcomers worked on the film. Abhay Sopori is a new composer and Sandesh Shandilya made a comeback with *Shikara*.

Anyway, I said no to the Sony team because I believe if you earn a lot of money without hard work, it corrupts the soul.

But let's get back to *Khamosh*. We didn't finish that story.

AJ: Of course! I believe you distributed *Khamosh* yourself. How did that come about?

VVC: One day I was walking with a crew member on Carter Road and he said:

> If you believe in your film, why don't you distribute *Khamosh* yourself?
> *Are you crazy? How would I do that?*

I was crazy enough to go and see Mr Manek Sidhwa, the owner of Regal cinema, and showed him *Khamosh*. He loved the film and agreed to let it run in his cinema for two weeks. We agreed to share the box-office takings fifty-fifty, and that's how unwittingly I became the distributor of my film.

I got hoardings made in Dadar and carried them in a truck to Regal. When the hoardings were put up, Binod Pradhan lit the cinema facade. This was all happening on a Thursday night and the next day the film opened with three shows: 3 p.m., 6 p.m. and 9 p.m. Binod, Renu and I sat in the balcony and watched the first-ever show of *Khamosh* in a cinema hall. There were a few people in the stalls but the hall was largely empty.

While we were watching the film, I suddenly felt it was too long. I furiously made some notes about the scenes we should cut. When the film was over, I gave Renu my notes and said: 'Let's edit these scenes out.' She refused point-blank to touch the film and said we had to wait at least a day. I started shouting at her, insisting she make the edits, but she absolutely refused and shouted back at me:

I won't touch it!
You will. I'm the producer!
I won't. I'm the editor.

To defuse the fireworks between us, Binod dragged Renu down to the cinema cafeteria. Before I could join them, I went to the loo where I saw five rough-looking guys. They had overheard me shouting and assumed I was connected to the film. As they were leaving, one of them turned to me and said: 'Why were you screaming? Are you the producer of the film?'

I didn't reply. Then he said loud and clear: 'Don't stress. Your night show is full.' I didn't know what the hell he was talking about. We went back into the cinema hall and watched the six o'clock show. The theatre was half-empty.

I was worried and went to the box-office counter after the 6 p.m. show to see if there were any advance bookings for the night show. There I read a notice stuck behind the glass counter—it said the 9 p.m. show was sold out!

Just before the night show started, I saw those same five guys outside Regal, selling tickets on the black; they were murmuring under their breath: 'Dus ka bees, dus ka bees . . .' [Twenty rupees for a ten-rupee ticket.] In those days, if ticket touts liked a film, they bought tickets in bulk and sold them for double the price just before the movie started. So the night show was houseful and instead of two weeks, *Khamosh* ran at Regal for six weeks!

I will always be grateful to those guys. One of them smiled at me while he was selling the tickets and said: 'I told you not to worry. Bola tha, na? Tension nahin lene ka.' [Told you not to stress.]

Manek Sidhwa, being the nice man that he was, kept *Khamosh* playing at Regal for some weeks and in that time I sold the film to other territories—Delhi, UP, Punjab, etc. I was finally a free man!

AJ: A free man?

VVC: Abhijat, the reason I was so anxious that *Khamosh* do well was I needed to pay back the loan of eight lakhs to the NFDC, which had funded the film. They were the only source of finance for us independent film-makers in those days. The commercial producers and financiers did not back us. If I had not returned the loan in full, the NFDC would refuse to fund my next movie and I would not have been able to make another film that easily.

I do not remember the exact process of our getting finance from the NFDC but I recall it was very interesting. I think we were given 75 per cent of the budget—in the case of *Khamosh*, it was eight lakhs. But we had to spend 25 per cent from our own resources before we could access the eight lakhs.

As you can imagine, we didn't have 25 per cent, which was about two lakhs. It was way beyond what we could manage. So we were obliged to request the actors to sign their contracts saying they had received their fees when it was not true. The actors trusted that I'd pay them if the film made any money. Once the actors signed, the signed contracts were sent to the NFDC as proof that we had spent the 25 per cent. The eight lakhs for production was then available.

So, you can understand why the stakes were very high for me. I had to make sure *Khamosh* made some money and the film go into profit so I could repay the NFDC loan and pay the actors who showed such faith in me.

AJ: I suppose there were many like you who worked in films out of a sense of passion and not just a desire to make money. And clearly, you were always crazy about the movies. I remember hearing about you growing a beard and roaming about a forest after you saw *Citizen Kane*. Did that really happen?

VVC: I'll tell you what happened—when I first went to the FTII, I arrived there with the impression I could be the best director in the world. I had seen many Hindi films and very few made any impression on me. I had this illusion that I could do as well, if not better than that. I believed once I had learnt the craft of film-making, I would go to Bombay and make great cinema.

You see, in my youth I mistakenly believed I was extraordinary, just because I had a first-class first degree in economics from Kashmir University and was a decent enough cricket player. I also felt important because my brother Vijay Praji, who headed the JAWA motorbike agency in Kashmir, would let me ride a new bike every week. I used to cruise the streets on the latest bike, noticed by everyone, especially young women. I felt so confident. It was all so innocent.

When my brother Chitranjan, who lived in London, heard I was going to film school, he gave me some of his used clothes. So I walked through those high FTII gates in Pune wearing an orange jacket, a flashy shirt and a green muffler. Everyone there thought I was joining the acting course and not the film direction classes. I was unbelievably cocky!

For the first few days, we had lectures on film theory and then they started showing us movies in a small classroom theatre. We started with Godard's *Breathless*. I was blown away. We saw *Breathless* in the morning and then at six o'clock that evening, we saw Orson Welles's *Citizen Kane*. After the screening, I asked everyone how old Orson Welles was when he made the film. They told me he was twenty-six or something. And as luck would have it, the last film of the day was Federico Fellini's *8½.*

After seeing those three amazing films—all in one day—I completely lost it. I was in an utterly conflicted state—elated on one hand because here was cinema I did not know existed, and equally depressed because I realized what an ass**le I had been for believing I was a great film-maker. I was nothing.

They say, 'You have to know a lot to know how little you know.' It was that kind of moment for me. I felt so small and couldn't sleep that night and couldn't get myself to shave the next day. So from a cocky idiot wearing an orange jacket, a flashy shirt and a green muffler, I grew a beard, put on a long Fab India cotton dressing gown and roamed around in a nearby forest trying to discover myself. I asked myself who and what the f*** I was. And should I be doing cinema at all?

The day we watched those three masterpieces completely changed me and I became a humble student of cinema. I knew I had a lot to learn and that's when I really started studying film in a serious way.

In those days, the only way you could see a movie was if you had access to the film print. There were no VHS tapes or DVDs, let alone being able to watch films on a mobile. Mr P.K. Nair, who was the founding director of the National Film Archives of India, was kind enough to recognize my enthusiasm and lent me a 16 mm print of *Breathless* so I could watch it on a Moviola and study the film's editing.

In *Breathless*, there's a famous scene in which Jean-Paul Belmondo and Jean Seberg are driving in a car through the streets of Paris. To advance the narrative, Godard used jump cuts. I had never seen a jump cut before. When I finally came to make *Khamosh*, I tried a jump cut in the scene where Naseeruddin Shah is hitting this guy in a swimming pool. He ducks him in and out of the water and suddenly a light falls on the faces of the two guys. Then I cut to floodlights being switched on further down the river. This way the two scenes are linked cinematically. I learnt this technique from Jean-Luc Godard.

Years later when I made *Broken Horses*, the first person I thanked was Mr P.K. Nair. He opened the doors of world cinema for us students.

AJ: And there's also your deep admiration for Orson Welles. I remember in 2015 when Welles's scripts of *Citizen Kane* were being auctioned, you bid for them.

VVC: Yes, I did, but someone in America who was richer outbid me. I would have loved to own his original scripts. The very fact a movie like *Citizen Kane* could be made, and that too in 1941, amazed me.

Let's say you're blind and you've never seen a beautiful sunset in your entire life and suddenly you get your eyesight and you see a sunset. *Citizen Kane* was like that for me. I was blind. Before that, I had mostly seen only Hindi movies. While I was watching *Citizen Kane*, I asked myself if I had died and gone to the heaven of cinema.

AJ: Much later, when you were already a very successful film director, you saw Milos Forman's *Amadeus* in the house of the director of photography Binod Pradhan, and you said how much the film moved you.

VVC: Oh, I just started weeping when Mozart is dying and tells Salieri: 'I'm tired. I'd like to rest a little bit.' The dialogue may not be exactly the way I remember it, but I know it made me weep.

Perhaps you don't know this, the other time I wept was watching a *Swan Lake* performance in Leningrad. I had gone to Russia with my film *Khamosh* and was a guest of the Soviet government. My Russian interpreter accompanied me to the ballet and when she saw me weeping at the end of the show, she got very worried and held my hand. I could not help but weep at such brilliance.

AJ: Many people think you're an arrogant man, but I have seen your humble and vulnerable side, especially in the face of great works of art and cinema. I'm thinking of the times you've spoken about David Lean and his work. Those sweeping long shots and top angles floored you.

VVC: I was a teenager when I first saw David Lean's *Lawrence of Arabia* and it just blew my mind. The film was playing at the Broadway in Srinagar and for days, I'd go back to see the film again and again. I mentioned Mr Vijay Dhar, the owner of the cinema, to you—well, he knew I had no money to buy a ticket, so he'd let me sit in the lobby in case there was an empty seat, and if there was one, he let me sneak in and watch the movie. That's how I managed to see *Lawrence of Arabia* dozens of times. I'll always be grateful to Mr Vijay Dhar.

I'll never forget the scene when Lawrence, having barely survived the Sinai desert crossing with Farraj, his young Arab attendant, comes to the British officers' club with Farraj and tells the barman: 'We want two large glasses of lemonade.' Everyone at the bar stares at them with disdain because Arabs are not allowed in the British officers' club. What an amazing scene.

I could not believe the scale of *Lawrence of Arabia*. Think of Omar Sharif's entry. He is just an indistinct shadowy figure on a camel till you see him emerge from the heat rising from the desert sand. The best entry ever. The film was like a dream to me. And Peter O'Toole was my cinema god. The way he walked on top of a train with his robe flying in the wind. He was regal; just majestic.

Remember how thrilled I was to meet Peter O'Toole? I'll cherish those moments forever. Abhijat, you were there too when we met him, weren't you?

AJ: Yes. We were flying back to Bombay from Rajasthan, where we were looking for locations for *Eklavya: The Royal Guard,* when we saw Peter O'Toole at the airport. Shantanu Moitra and Swanand Kirkire were with us too. As we were about to board the plane, you went up to Peter O'Toole and introduced yourself. You told him you were a film-maker and how much you loved *Lawrence of Arabia* and just before he entered the plane you added: 'During the flight, we'll get you two large glasses of lemonade.' Then I quoted a line from *Beckett*: 'Well played, Thomas.' Peter O'Toole looked at me and said: 'That was forty-one years ago.'

VVC: What a wonderful chance meeting. We talked throughout the flight and the affection we felt for each other was immediate. I gave Peter my phone number but wasn't sure we'd ever meet again. As we were getting into the bus that took us from the plane to the terminal, he almost took a stumble. When I caught him from falling, Peter said: 'I was only acting!' And I instantly replied: 'And I was only directing, Peter.' [*laughs*] I think that was the beginning of our friendship.

Then to my great surprise, he called me that same night and asked whether we could meet for dinner.

Sure, Peter, you must come over.
Yes, but not too many people.
Don't worry, there's nobody in this city who really likes me, so dinner will be very exclusive! There'll only be you and me.

He came home that night for dinner. He even taught my son Agni how to play cricket. Peter said he was an MCC instructor. He bowled while Agni learnt how to bat. My son was fascinated by his MCC coach. When Peter returned to London, he sent a tape of Brian Lara for Agni and a letter that's framed and hanging on the wall of my son's room. It was a touching letter that reads: 'Dear Agni, I can teach you how to defend but I can't teach you how to attack. That must come from your own heart. Watch this chap on DVD, Lara. He is a left-hander too.'

One day when Agni was very young, he came running to me and said: 'Dad, my coach is on TV. Come quickly!' I ran into the other room and *Lawrence of Arabia* was on. I laughed and told my son: 'That's Peter O'Toole, you idiot!'

AJ: Peter also told us a wonderful and poignant story about Keith Miller. All cricket fans will know that Keith Miller was a great all-rounder in the same league as Gary Sobers.

Miller had been inducted in the Hall of Fame at the MCG in 1996 and immortalized in a bronze statue. Keith Miller sent Peter O'Toole a postcard with only these words: 'Mate, we are bronzed!'

Sadly, Peter received this postcard from Australia a few days after Miller had passed away.

VVC: Peter was such a great guy. When Peter came to our place for dinner, I told him I wasn't from a well-to-do family and my father, being an honest man, was poor, but I once had this dream of going to the Royal Academy of Dramatic Art, RADA, in London. I told him I had saved up the equivalent of a pound in rupees when I was a kid and had ordered the RADA prospectus. The day it arrived in the post, I held it in my hands, knowing that it had come all the way from London. I read it from cover to cover. I knew it was the closest I'd ever get to RADA. Peter heard me out and that was the end of it.

During my next trip to London, Peter invited me for dinner at a restaurant. After dinner, he said in that very British accent of his: 'Would you like to take a little stroll, Vinod?' So we left the restaurant. I could sense he was not strolling aimlessly, but walked with purpose. When we got to a building on Gower Street, he asked me to follow him inside. I had no idea where we were. When we entered the hall, I still remember there was a wooden staircase and on the walls hung portraits of many famous actors, including Peter O'Toole. He looked at me and said: 'This is RADA. This is where you dreamed of coming.'

I held on to the banister and wept like a baby, saying: 'You know, if someone had ever told me that one day "Lawrence of Arabia" would take me to visit RADA, I'd never have believed them, Peter.'

Two dreams came together for me that evening.

AJ: I can understand how you must've felt. I'm curious to know—why did you want to go to RADA? It's a school for actors. Were you keen on becoming an actor?

VVC: When I was obsessed with RADA, I didn't even know it was an acting school. But one thing I knew, I could never actually go there. I was just dreaming of getting a great education.

You know, when you're raised in a small mohalla you have big dreams of going to London and studying. I was basically very confused. I didn't know whether I wanted to be Dilip Kumar or Mehboob Khan. I just wanted to be in the movies. But I knew I couldn't really act. When I saw myself in *Murder at Monkey Hill*, I thought my acting was shitty.

Amol Palekar insisted on casting me in his film *Ankahee,* where I played a character called Patwardhan. It was fun, but I felt like a puppet. Then there was the bit part as Dushasana in *Jaane Bhi Do Yaaro.*

AJ: How did you come to act in Kundan Shah's film?

VVC: It was a save-the-day situation. Kundan Shah was in my class at the FTII. Renu, he and I spent time together towards the end of my third year in Pune and then in Bombay we met often. He used to live in Sion.

One day, Ravi Malik, who looked after the financing of independent small-budget films at the NFDC, called me. Kundan's script had been approved by the script committee and Ravi said: 'I'm hesitant to give the money to Kundan Shah because, knowing him, he'll go over budget. If you work as his production controller, I'll happily finance the film.'

That's how I became the production controller on *Jaane Bhi Do Yaaro*. Renu edited the movie and Kundan had the help of a very close-knit group of friends. My job was to get the film done within budget. To save money I even did about eight or nine walk-on parts.

For the climax scene, I had hired an actor to play Dushasana for 500 rupees a day—or a total of 2000 for four days. On the day of the shoot, the actor arrived and said: 'I'm charging 2000 a day. Not 500 rupees.'

While we were talking, I was informed the shot was ready and then one of the assistants arrived with Dushasana's costume and stood there. The actor and I continued negotiating. He was sure I had no other option and I would have to agree to his terms, so he repeated:

I won't do it for less than 2000 a day.
Yaar, we talked about 500 a day. Or 2000 for four days.
Okay, take a thousand a day. Now get your costume on.
No.
Okay, take 1500. The shot's ready. The costume's here. Done?
No, sir.

I looked at the assistant and said: 'Give me that f***ing costume!' I took off my clothes and put on Dushasana's costume. The actor got flustered and asked:

Sir, what are you doing?
Forget it now.
Okay, I'll do it for 500 a day.
It's a done deal.

We shook hands and I said: 'Now you give me 500 rupees a day if you want the part!'

That fellow didn't know what to say. Dressed in Dushasana's costume, I marched onto the set. Kundan looked at me and couldn't understand why the f*** I was standing in front of him in full costume.

Yaar, what the hell are you doing?
Just shoot, yaar! It's a budget-related problem. Not your problem!

That foolish actor was blackmailing me because he knew his shot was ready and thought I was cornered. That's how I came to act in that hilarious climax.

AJ: You've often said film-makers must make their films on budget and that was one of our greatest strengths—we worked within budget.

VVC: The point is, Abhijat, if we want to make films we believe in, they have to be within a certain budget. It's all about how much you spend on a movie. When you spend hundreds of crores, there'll be pressure on you to recover the investment, so you'll have to appeal to the lowest common denominator.

People are greedy. Everyone wants to make as much money as they can. They love mediocrity because it often results in box-office success. But if you want to maintain a certain standard, stay within budget. There's no other way to make good films.

AJ: You said you admired directors like Fellini, Coppola, Welles and Hitchcock, and you also admired popular films like *Mother India* and *Mughal-e-Azam*. But when it came to deciding which path to choose, you decided to blend both cinematic traditions. That blending was evident to me in *Parinda*.

VVC: Your saying that reminds of the mythical tale of a demon whose memory was stored in the brain of a parrot. Many tried to slay the demon but they all failed. When they realized the parrot was the demon's memory, they killed the parrot and the demon forgot that he was a demon.

Abhijat, with your memory I think you're my sacred parrot! I don't remember half the things that have happened in my life, but you do. [*both laugh*]

AJ: [*smiles*] Let's not rely on my memory alone and go back to the time before we met. That was a really tough period for you, wasn't it?

VVC: [*long pause*] After the release of *Sazaye Maut*, when I was writing *Khamosh*, I was totally down and out. So I went to Khandala with my dialogue writer Ranjit Kapoor and his girlfriend Madhu. We stayed in a modest little hotel and thought we'd try and write the script there.

But I could not focus and felt it was all pointless. I didn't know which way to turn, or what I should do—what kind of films I should make. Should I forget about film-making altogether? I was so down that one night I walked out of that small hotel room, planning to end my life. Nothing felt worth it. I felt I didn't fit in anyway.

I walked to the main Bombay–Pune highway and stood there. Huge lorries were zipping past me at high speed with their horns blaring and their blinding headlights hurting my eyes. It was about 2 a.m. All I had to do to end it all was step onto the fast lane and a truck would have easily hit me. I was so close to doing it. But what stopped me? The simple answer was my love for my family, my mother, my brother Vir. I thought it would be terrible for them. It was the love for my family that made me stop and slowly walk back to the hotel.

As usual, the next morning, I woke up when my alarm went off at nine. I didn't know that Ranjit and Madhu had set the clock back two hours and it was actually 11 a.m. They put the clock back because they felt I needed to rest.

To this day, Ranjit and Madhu have no idea that I had come that close to ending my life. When you're down and out and depressed, you feel it's the end of the road and you can't take it any more, but don't ever think about ending your life. When I look back and see what a full life I've had, what a waste it would've been if I had taken just that one step onto that highway. It would've been the dumbest thing I would have ever done.

AJ: Oh, I didn't know about this. I've always thought of you as a survivor.

VVC: You know, Abhijat, after that night I came to the realization that there are only three kinds of real problems in life—one is health. If health is a problem, it's a real problem. The second is dire poverty. I'm talking about the kind of poverty where you don't have enough money to feed yourself or your family, where poverty can threaten your very survival. And the third problem, which is critical, is a created problem. Problems that we create for ourselves. So if you analyse the problems we face, you'll find 95 per cent are actually created or imagined; because true problems really concern health and living in dire poverty. Thinking of life in this way has helped me to face very difficult times. I see this as my three-point mantra.

AJ: But I know how tough it was for you to lead life on your terms and make the movies you wanted to make.

VVC: Even trying to release *Khamosh* was tough. No one was willing to help me. I had to think what my options were. I could have gone from one film festival to another with a begging bowl, hoping I'd get some sort of break. Or I could have approached some established producers and asked for their backing, but that would have come with many strings attached. I'm not saying these were bad choices in themselves but they were less desirable.

I went through a huge amount of stress, and felt years of my life had been wasted just trying to get *Khamosh* into the theatres.

AJ: You didn't get much support from the film industry, but as you said, Vir-ji, your brother, encouraged you throughout. And in the light of your relationship with him, perhaps this bond between brothers transformed itself into a recurrent theme in your movies. It's there in *Parinda, Broken Horses* and even suggested in *Eklavya.*

VVC: You may be right. I've always been very close to Vir and still am.

Vir supported me from the day I went to the FTII. In those days, he was earning a salary of just over 1100 rupees a month and out of that he paid 250 for my fees. If he didn't have a job at the time, there was no way I could have gone to film school. Since I had topped the Kashmir University in economics, and was named the National Scholar of India, I got a scholarship of 200 rupees a month. That was the money I used to feed myself . . . Rs 200.

AJ: Did you ever think of returning all the money that Vir spent on you?

VVC: [*smiles*] That reminds me—when my first wife Renu Saluja and I were holidaying in Kashmir many years ago and we needed some money, I kept telling her: 'Don't worry. I'll borrow something from Vir.' She asked with great concern: 'How will we return all this money you're borrowing?' I started laughing and said:

I'm never going to return it.
But you're borrowing it?
No, what I mean is I'm taking it. I'm not borrowing it.

Renu believed if you borrowed money, you had to return it. While I was just using the word 'borrow' as a manner of speech. It never struck me that I had to return Vir's money.

AJ: Tell me how you met Renu Saluja.

VVC: I was at the FTII for about a year when she joined. Word went round that Renu was the actress Radha Saluja's sister, so I was full of disdain. I thought she would be the filmi type. When we started working together, I got to know her.

We got married when I was in my early twenties. Renu was six months older to me. My father thought I was too young to marry. Just think of it! My son is that age now and if he told me he wanted to get married, I'd ask him if he had lost his mind! No wonder my father thought I was nuts.

There was great resistance to our marriage from both our families. Renu's mother freaked out. When I told Renu I was Ramanand Sagar's brother, her mother didn't believe my shit and called Ramanand Sagar:

There's this rascal at the FTII who is going around lying
and saying he's your brother. Please report him to the
police and have him arrested.
What's the boy's name?
Some Vinod Chopra from Kashmir.
How can I have him arrested? That rascal from Kashmir
is my brother.

[*both laugh*] I wanted us to live together but we couldn't
because it wasn't done in those days. So Renu and I
decided to get married. Her parents continued to object
and definitely did not want us to get married in their home.
They lived in an army bungalow in Colaba and were not
keen that their neighbours find out their daughter was
marrying a nobody. To save them embarrassment, Renu's
father, Colonel H.L. Saluja, and his wife asked one of their
friends to let us marry in their flat. Their friends thankfully
agreed and they gave us their address in Colaba. My
parents were not happy about the marriage either, but they
came to Bombay.

There was my father, mother and me sitting in a car
driving towards Colaba on my wedding day. My mother
insisted on covering my face with a sehra. We drove around
in circles trying to find the building. We stopped and asked
people on the road, but no one knew where it was. Finally,
at one point, I had to get out of the car, lift my sehra off
my face and ask a paanwallah: 'Ye building kahaan hai?'
[Where is this building?]

The paanwallah couldn't stop laughing! He thought the
situation was hilarious and said: 'Where's this building? You

mean you're getting married and you don't know where? Sit in the car, I'll come with you and show you where you have to go.'

The whole situation felt unreal. It was a bit like a scene in a Kundan Shah comedy! When we finally got to the flat, I rang the bell and Renu, who never wore any make-up, opened the door. There she stood, with make-up and all, looking just like a Bengali bride. She looked so strange. We both started laughing. If you see our marriage photo, I looked like such a kid.

Sometime later, I remember we joined a yoga class and when Renu couldn't come with me one day, the yoga teacher asked: 'Didi nahin aayi aaj?' [Your sister didn't come today?] I didn't have the heart to tell him she wasn't my sister but my wife. It did not occur to the yoga teacher that we could be husband and wife.

Cinema was our passion. We lived and breathed cinema. It's important when you start your career to have a partner who shares the same passion for something that means a lot to you. Renu and I worked very closely together. We fought a lot too, mostly about editing. There were times when she got furious and threw film cans at me. She was brilliant and I was lucky to have her in my life when I was making my way in films. But I wanted kids and she did not want any. And that was one of the many reasons why we got divorced in 1983. We had a lawyer friend and he helped us to file for divorce.

AJ: You must tell us about the divorce proceedings. They seemed most unusual to me. [*smiles*]

VVC, a rebel in the making. Kashmir, 1950s.

Since they were children, VVC has shared a close relationship with his only sister, Shelly. Kashmir, 1950s.

VVC's parents were the pillars of his formative years. Mrs Shanti Devi Chopra and Shri Dinanath Chopra. New Delhi, 1964.

VVC's father, Shri Dinanath Chopra, was a great storyteller and a man of immense integrity.
Kashmir, 1970s.

The extended Chopra family gathered together to celebrate Shri Dinanath Chopra's and Mrs Shanti Devi Chopra's visit to Europe, their first trip overseas. (*l to r*) Mrs Leela Sagar, Ramanand Sagar, Vir Chopra, Shri Dinanath Chopra, Vidhu Vinod Chopra, Mrs Shanti Devi Chopra, Subhash Sagar and guests. Bombay airport, 1970s.

चौबीसवां Twenty Fourth
राष्ट्रीय National
फिल्म समारोह Film Festival
1977 1977

प्रमाण-पत्र Certificate

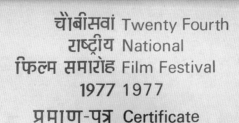

चल-चित्र   मरडर ऐट मंकी हिल [हिन्दी]
Film   *Murder at Monkey Hill [Hindi]*

श्रेणी   सर्वोत्तम प्रयोगात्मक फिल्म
Category   *Best Experimental Film*

पुरस्कार विजेता   निर्देशक :- श्री विनोद चोपड़ा
Award Winner   *Director :- Shri Vinod Chopra*

पुरस्कार   "रजत कमल" तथा रु० 4,000/- नकद पुरस्कार
Award   *"Rajat Kamal" & Cash Prize of Rs 4,000/-*
    [Rupees Four Thousand]

सचिव
Secretary
सूचना और प्रसारण मंत्रालय,
भारत सरकार, नई दिल्ली
Ministry of Information and Broadcasting,
Government of India, New Delhi

nff

National Award Certificate for *Murder at Monkey Hill*. VVC's tussle with Shri L.K. Advani over the 4000-rupee cash prize mentioned in this certificate resulted in a lifelong friendship.

FD film named
for academy award

Films Division's documentary "An Encounter with Faces" has been nominated for the short sub-ject award of the 51st Annual Academy Awards, California.

This short film attempts to bring awareness among the people the condition of the delinquent child-ren, their problems and the need for their rehabilitation.

The film has been produced by Mr. K. K. Kapil, joint chief pro-ducer of the Films Division and di-rected by Mr. Vinod Chopra.

This film has won the Golden Peacock at the 7th International Film Festival held recently in New Delhi.

Traders' assn.

By A Staff Reporter

Industrialists representing 70 units in the Taloja-Panvel indus-tri

VVC discovered that his film *An Encounter with Faces* had been nominated for an Oscar through this small news item published in the middle pages of the *Times of India*.

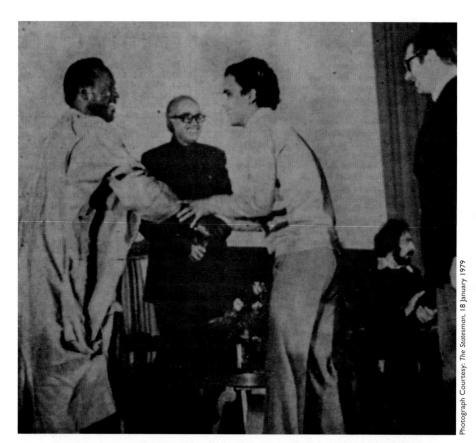

Photograph Courtesy: *The Statesman*, 18 January 1979

Receiving the Golden Peacock Award for *An Encounter with Faces*. This is the photograph VVC showed to the American embassy official to get his visa to attend the Academy Awards. (*l to r*) With Ousmane Sembene, Shri L.K. Advani, unidentified jury member and Krzysztof Zanussi.

VVC remembers: 'If you look at our wedding photo, I looked like such a kid!' Mumbai, August 1977.

1st. Sept. to 4th Sept. — 1976.

FEATURE FILMS

1. Amitabh — 4th sept. onwards.

(2 x Manoj. 3 . x Yash Chopra.)
4 x Hrishi da/either or 5. (what do you say?) *
                                    6th sept. 76.

4th Sept. onwards. to 30th Sept. (or end oct.)
          — for acting : understood probability ratio 2% or less.

1. / Hrishi da .

2. Gulzar .

3. Rajshree productions .

4 x ~~Shyam Benegal~~ — D (2 short films.)

5 Basu Chaterjee .

6. Sunil Dutt — D .

7. B. R. Chopra .

8 x ~~B R Ishara~~ **Navketan** .

(9.10.11. ~~Hrrucan~~ — ~~K. A. Abbas~~ — ~~R. Singh Dade~~ .)

either/or . SHORT FILMS .
1st oct. onwards.

1. films Division — 8th sept.

2. H. Thompson.

3. Saeed + mani kaul — 8th sept.

4. Shyam Benegal .

5. Etc. Etc.

The Wish List penned by Renu Saluja and VVC shows that making a film with Amitabh Bachchan was their top priority. Mahabaleshwar, September 1976.

The concept poster sketches of *Prashant* that VVC showed Amitabh Bachchan while pitching the film to him. Late 1970s.

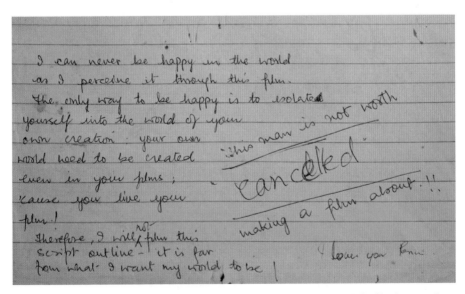

Despite getting a chance to work with the superstar, VVC decided to cancel the film because the character of 'Prashant' didn't work. Years later, when this book was being written, VVC saw, for the first time ever, that Renu Saluja had scribbled 'I love you' at the bottom of the page.

VVC's feature film debut, *Sazaye Maut*, was made on a budget of just $6000. With Naseeruddin Shah. Mahabaleshwar, 1980s.

Since the crew could not afford proper equipment, all trolley shots in *Sazaye Maut* were taken from this car. Mahabaleshwar, 1980s.

A close and timeless relationship between the Chopra brothers was the original inspiration for *Parinda*. With Vir Chopra. Kashmir, late 1960s.

The brothers in Spain, 2010s.

Unconventional storytelling and filming methods gave *Parinda* (1989) a cult status in the decades that followed its release. (*l to r*) Renu Saluja (standing at the back), Binod Pradhan (behind the camera), Vidhu Vinod Chopra (wearing a cap) and other crew members. Mumbai, 1980s.

VVC's mother came to Mumbai for the premiere of *Parinda* in 1989. She intended to stay for a week—but communal trouble erupted in Kashmir, leading to the exodus of hundreds of thousands of Kashmiri Pandits. As a result, she could never go back home again. With (*l to r*) Col H.L. Saluja (Renu Saluja's father), Ramanand Sagar, Shabnam Sukhdev, Vidhu Vinod Chopra, Mrs Shanti Devi Chopra and Vir Chopra. Mumbai, 1989.

Nana Patekar's role in *Parinda* revolutionized the way villains were portrayed in Indian cinema.

His performance in *Parinda* gave Jackie Shroff his first *Filmfare* Best Actor Award. With Madhuri Dixit and Anil Kapoor. Mumbai, 1980s.

Anil Kapoor was seen with short hair for the first time in his career in the iconic saga *1942: A Love Story*. Dalhousie, 1991.

VVC explains a shot to Renu Saluja as Anil Kapoor listens intently. On the sets of *1942: A Love Story*. Mumbai, 1992.

VVC makes it a point to go to his hometown once every year. With his daughter Ishaa Chopra in Gulmarg, Kashmir, 2002.

Another one of his annual Kashmir trips. With his family—Anupama Chopra, Zuni Chopra and Agni Dev Chopra. Kashmir, 2004.

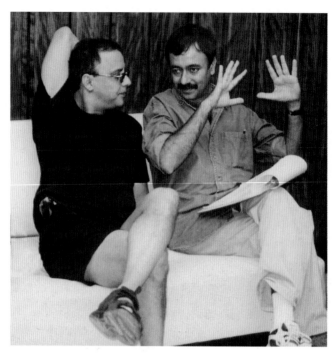

With close collaborator, Rajkumar Hirani, discussing the script of *Munna Bhai M.B.B.S.*, the first film VVC produced. Mumbai, 2001.

Pradeep Sarkar, Rajkumar Hirani and VVC share a laugh during the pre-production of *Shikara*. Mumbai, 2018.

Sanjay Dutt talking through a scene with VVC during the filming of *Munna Bhai M.B.B.S.*
Mumbai, early 2000s.

After *Munna Bhai M.B.B.S.*, Sanjay Dutt transformed himself into a Bengali for *Parineeta*. With
(*l to r*) Pradeep Sarkar and Rajkumar Hirani.

Following dinner together, Peter O'Toole took VVC on a surprise visit to the Royal Academy of Dramatic Art (RADA). With (*l to r*) Anupama Chopra, Shelly Dhar and Subhash Dhar. London, 2000s.

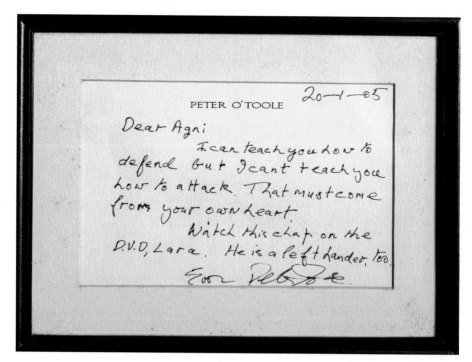

PETER O'TOOLE   20—1—05

Dear Agni
        I can teach you how to defend but I cant teach you how to attack. That must come from your own heart
        Watch this chap on the D.V.D, Lara. He is a left hander, too.
                Your Peter O'Toole

Peter O'Toole's letter to Agni Dev Chopra still hangs on his bedroom wall.

Dr. RAMANAND SAGAR, D.Lit.
Awarded **PADMASHRI** by President of India

Dear Vidu,

Congratulation for the National

Award.

You have made everyone

proud of you.

You brought Fame to the Family

अपनों कहते हैं

[बालदान का चिराग]

Love from both of us.

Yours Lovingly

Sagar

3.2.2005.

Res.: Sagar Villa, Road No.12-A, J.V.P.D. Scheme, Mumbai 400049, India.
Phone: 26184315 • Fax: +91-22-26155479
Office: Natraj Studios, 194 Andheri-Kurla Road, Andheri (East), Mumbai 400069, India.
Phone: 26830881, 26834707, 26833473 • Fax: +91-22-26831002 • E-mail: rsagar@sagararts.com

Ramanand Sagar's letter to VVC after he had won another National Award.

The day Amitabh Bachchan reached the location at 5 a.m. When asked why he had come an hour early, Bachchan said: 'Because I don't like to be shouted at for being late.' With Saif Ali Khan during the shoot of *Eklavya*. Udaipur, 2006.

VVC smiles as Amitabh Bachchan explains why he always sits on stacked chairs. Udaipur, 2006.

VVC—the 4th idiot. With (*l to r*) Sharman Joshi, Aamir Khan and R. Madhavan during the promotion of *3 Idiots*. Mumbai, 2009.

With *Broken Horses*, VVC finally got to work in Hollywood. With (*l to r*) Nicholas Mastandrea (assistant director), Abhijat Joshi (standing behind), unidentified crew member, Tom Stern (cinematographer) and Peter Rosenfeld (steadicam operator). New Mexico, 2014.

VVC had to learn new ways of directing actors as the American cast he worked with in *Broken Horses* belonged to a different tradition than the Indian actors he had previously directed. (*l to r*) Anton Yelchin, Vincent D'Onofrio and Chris Marquette.

Peter Rosenfeld holds a director's viewfinder for VVC as he frames a shot. With Tom Stern (standing in the back, left) and other crew members. California, 2014.

The meeting that turned into a friendship. With film-maker James Cameron and actor Aamir Khan at the India Today Conclave. New Delhi, 2010.

VVC and Alfonso Cuarón met as jury members at the Prague International Film Festival in 1994. Picture taken at one of the early *Broken Horses* screenings. London, 2015.

With his security guards during the filming of *Shikara*. Kashmir, March 2018.

Thousands of Kashmiri Pandits came together to help VVC make India's first feature film on their exodus. During the filming of *Shikara* in Jammu, April 2018.

Filming the final scene of *Shikara*. Taj Mahal, Agra, October 2018.

A light moment shared during a special screening of *Shikara*. With (*l to r*) Pratibha Advani, Vir Chopra, Shri L.K. Advani and Anupama Chopra. New Delhi, February 2020.

The coconut tree outside VVC's home. Every time he looks at it, he is reminded of the train journeys he used to take to this city of dreams when he was younger. Agni Dev Chopra and Zuni Chopra. Maria Cottage, Mumbai, 2020.

VVC scribbled 'We are impermanent like this writing' on a Buddha Board and watched as the words disappeared forever. Mumbai, 2020.

VVC: In those days divorces took place in the main court; there were no family courts. Renu and I stood in front of the judge and he asked me some question. I didn't remember the answer so I turned to Renu to help me out. The judge was completely mystified.

Why are you asking her?
Sir, I have a bad memory and she remembers everything.
So how will you live without her?
We've decided to get divorced but we'll stay friends.
No, no. You look so good together. Please don't consider divorce. Think it over and come back in six months.

The judge could see we were good friends and so he refused to grant us a divorce. Six months later, we went back to the same court and the same judge was there. This time we stood apart and did not smile at each other. I told the judge: 'We're enemies now. We want a divorce.' With a smile on his face, he said: 'I've never met a couple like you.'

Our lawyer explained we wanted a divorce by mutual consent. It was an unusual divorce because we were clearly very friendly with one another, so naturally the judge got confused.

Even after we had divorced, Renu remained an essential part of my team and there was no question of anyone else editing my films. Her passing was totally devastating. She was my best friend.

AJ: Then you got married again.

VVC: A few years later, I married the film-maker Shabnam Sukhdev. We have a lovely daughter—Ishaa. Shabnam raised her and they live in Canada now. Our marriage didn't last and for years I thought I'd never marry again.

AJ: I want us to talk about your personal life a bit later, but for the moment can we talk about *Parinda*, the film that set you apart as a film-maker in India?

Parinda has themes of brotherhood, betrayal, lost values and valour. You cast the top stars of the time, including Anil Kapoor, Jackie Shroff, Madhuri Dixit and Nana Patekar. How did you go about developing the screenplay?

VVC: The first lines I wrote were the most commercial and clichéd lines I could think of. Two young brothers come to Bombay. The younger brother is crying because he's hungry and the elder brother tells him: 'Don't cry. I'm your brother. I'll protect you.'

When I was writing the script, I reminded myself about what François Truffaut once said. These are not his exact words, I'm paraphrasing but he said something like: 'I build the edifice of my film using the pillars of commercial cinema and then one by one, I knock the pillars down. And if the edifice still holds, I know I have a script.'

So bearing his words in mind I took a smuggler, two brothers, a murdered friend and used all the elements of a popular Hindi movie and built my edifice. One by one, I turned the old stereotypes and clichés of the Hindi film on their heads.

Take villains—they were mostly stereotypes in popular cinema. Many bad guys were smugglers who wore suits and ties and travelled in Impalas. The zamindars were the bad guys before the city villain took over. By the 1980s, the westernized bad guy had become very popular.

So, in *Parinda*, I went for a different kind of villain— Anna, who was played by Nana Patekar. Anna is an unusual villain who wore kurta-pyjamas and kolhapuri chappals. He didn't fit the image of the typical villain. Even the way Anil Kapoor and Jackie Shroff were dressed in the film was unusual. It was rare to see Hindi film stars wearing simple jeans and ordinary shirts during that era.

That reminds me of a funny incident. Anil Kapoor and Jackie Shroff were filming with me one day and the scene required Jackie to wear a lungi. That evening they had to go to some filmi party and decided to change on the set instead of rushing home and out again. When they came to say goodbye to me, I was taken aback by how smart they looked and said: 'You guys look like real stars, man!' Jackie retorted: 'F*** you! We *are* stars.'

We all laughed. I had completely forgotten I was directing two of the biggest stars of the time. To me they were my characters, Kishen and Karan.

AJ: The opening sequence of *Parinda* has many shots that reminded me of Hitchcock and even the opening music is very Hitchcockian. You said you made the film on a tight budget and I believe the car Jackie Shroff drove in the film was his own. Is that right?

VVC: Yes, that's right. We used Jackie's black Fiat and he wore his own jeans in the movie.

AJ: Some critics thought his black car represented the character's dark side.

VVC: That's what some critics said! We used his black Fiat because we couldn't afford to hire another car. A lot of people interpreted it as representing the dark side of the character, but if he had a red car, we'd have used that instead. No doubt someone would've come up with another fancy interpretation.

AJ: You told me that after you wrote the first draft of *Parinda*, you gave the script to Vir-ji to read and he said he loved the first act, but didn't like the second half, so you rewrote it. Is that true?

VVC: Yes. In the original second half, Iqbal Langda [Sameer Khakhar] teaches Karan [Anil Kapoor] how to shoot. He trains him so that when Karan returns to Bombay he can seek revenge. But Karan is not a violent man, he's just someone trapped in bad circumstances and you could say he's forced to go with the flow. My brother was right, the second half needed fixing.

AJ: What about the casting of *Parinda*? How did you find your actors?

VVC: I saw a Marathi play called *Purush* with Nana Patekar at the Shivaji Natya Mandir in Dadar, and thought he was a fascinating performer. I asked him to come on board and he happily agreed.

The casting process was very convoluted. After *Khamosh*, I wanted to work with stars. Anil Kapoor was a big star at that time and he was keen to do different kinds of roles and he still is. He was my first choice to play Karan, one of the brothers. I wanted Nana to play Kishen, the other brother, a role that Jackie Shroff ultimately played. Dimple Kapadia was going to play Paro, the part that went to Madhuri Dixit, and Anupam Kher was initially cast as Anna, the gangster. The original casting was very bad. But luck was on my side when Anil Kapoor said: 'I don't think I can act as Nana's brother.'

He said this over dinner. I didn't realize it was his way of saying he wanted out. Anil's wife, Sunita, later told me he would not work on the film. I understood what Anil was actually saying—either drop Nana or he was out. I was a week away from the start of the shoot and couldn't drop Nana Patekar as a matter of principle, so the shooting was stalled.

I was sure no one would think I took a principled stand by sticking by Nana; they would probably assume Anil had decided to walk out of the film. So I went to Naseer and tried to cast him, but that didn't work out. The whole casting story became too complicated and I just let everything stop. My crew and I bought a cricket bat and we played cricket for days. Nana joined us and we had good fun.

AJ: R.D. Burman was your composer of choice for *Parinda*, wasn't he?

VVC: I'll share another memory with you that says a lot about R.D. Burman.

He was going to record the song 'Pyar ke mod pe' — that's when Anil Kapoor walked away from the movie, so I had no money. I asked R.D. Burman to cancel the song recording. He asked why and I explained the situation to him. Dada said something I'll never forget:

> Tu kal aa jaana Film Center. Mere gaane ki recording hai, tu aayega toh maza aayega. [Come to Film Center tomorrow. I have a song recording. It'll be fun if you come.]
> *Dada, I won't make it. I'm too busy handling this mess.*
> Meri ek film hai, *Parinda*, uska gaana main record kar raha hoon. [I'm composing music for a film called *Parinda*. Tomorrow I'll be recording a song for the movie.]

Dada paid for the recording from his own pocket. That was R.D. Burman for you.

AJ: When Anil Kapoor opted out of *Parinda*, what happened then?

VVC: It was soon clear that Naseer was not interested because he thought Anil's role was the main role and I couldn't make him understand that the role I was offering him was just as important. Also, as I mentioned before, we had no money to pay the actors before the shoot and it was risky for them, because if the film flopped they'd never get paid.

Naseer told me to go to Jackie Shroff and see if he'd agree to sign the NFDC contract without actually receiving any payment. I said: 'I'll persuade him to sign.' Naseer smiled and added: 'You may persuade him to sign, but how will you persuade him to act?'

In my anger and frustration, I went to meet Jackie Shroff. He had become a big star by then and was shooting near Mount Mary Church. Anil Kapoor had told him about *Parinda* and Jackie seemed interested in us working together.

I was living in a tiny flat in Kalpana Apartments in Bandra and Jackie came home that night. He spent hours reading the script and when he finished, he got up and said: 'Kidhar sign karna hai?' [Where do I sign?]

He knew the terms of the NFDC contract and just signed it and added: 'There's only one problem. I can't act.' [*both laugh*]

It was something I already knew. People had warned me that he couldn't hit his mark. It was a running joke in the industry. It was even rumoured that when shooting *Hero*, Subhash Ghai would have to tell Jackie to look left and then right.

When Jackie said he couldn't act, I assured him I'd give him a mantra and if he read it every morning, he'd have no problem acting. He thought I was talking nonsense but I insisted the mantra would work. I went into my bedroom and wrote something on a bit of paper, put it into an envelope and gave it to Jackie, saying: 'Repeat the mantra a hundred times. But don't open the envelope now. It's sacred. Open it tomorrow morning.'

He took the envelope and a few hours later he called me from his landline at home and said: 'F*** you!' Because the words I had written in capital letters were just: 'I CAN ACT!' [*both laugh*]

That was the beginning of our great friendship.

AJ: You told me another funny story about Jackie visiting you very late one night.

VVC: Yeah, he was supposed to come to my place at 10 p.m. for rehearsals. But he didn't turn up till 1 a.m. He walks in and is laughing like a kid and says: 'Shut the door! Hurry! I was late and knew you'd abuse me so I brought you some roses to calm you down. But I went to the wrong floor and pressed the doorbell. Your neighbour peeped through the keyhole and opened the door. She was grinning from ear to ear to see me standing there with roses. I realized my blunder, but didn't know what to do or say, so I handed her the flowers and ran down the stairs.'

I couldn't stop laughing. The man had gone to the wrong floor. The next morning when my neighbour, a simple housewife, came over, she raved on about Jackie the star appearing at her door past midnight with red roses for her. She thought it was a dream and only when she saw the roses in a vase sitting on her table the next morning, did she know it had really happened. It was crazy.

AJ: How was it working with Jackie?

VVC: I remember Jackie's first day on set—everyone calls him Jaggu—I told my cinematographer, Binod Pradhan, to go for bounce lighting and light the whole set, so Jackie would not need any marks and could deliver his lines anywhere on the set. When he arrived, as expected, he said:

Okay, very good. I read the scene as you requested. Now where's my mark?
Jaggu, you can start anywhere you like.
What do you mean 'anywhere'? Give me a mark.
You decide how you want to start the scene.

He gave me one of those Jackie Shroff stares and asked me again about his mark. Binod Pradhan, who was always calm and quiet, added: 'There *is* no mark, Jaggu. You can start the scene anywhere.'

That's when Jackie started hurling abuse at us: 'What the f*** did you guys learn at film school? Is this cinema or what? You call this direction? Directors have to tell us actors where to stand and how to look and what to do. What film course did you do? Bloody hell! You're asking me to decide. It's not my job.'

He was screaming like a madman. I told him calmly to do whatever felt natural to him. He swore at me, stormed off the set and came back half an hour later and said in a calm voice: 'Is it okay if I start the scene by looking out of the window as though I'm waiting for my brother?'

That was the beginning of Jackie Shroff, the actor. He went on to win *Filmfare*'s Best Actor award in 1990 for *Parinda*.

AJ: His performance was a revelation for everyone.
I recall something about some sort of scar for his face.

VVC: Such a waste of money, man! Fifteen thousand rupees! There was a Parsi gentleman in town who used to do special make-up. I went through hell getting that scar. Jackie's face was perfect, so I thought a scar would make him look more interesting—like a blot on the face of the moon.

On the first day of the shoot, it took Jackie an hour to have his make-up done, scar and all. Just before the camera started rolling, I looked through the lens, walked up to him and ripped the bloody scar off his face, threw it on the floor and said: 'There! It's gone.'

The scar looked totally fake. Fifteen thousand bucks gathered dust on the floor that day. [*both laugh*]

AJ: The entry of the hero is always important, especially in Indian cinema, and I recall you wanted to make an elaborate set for Jackie's entry, but it was beyond your budget.

VVC: Budget! What budget? You won't believe it, but we had to make the whole film in twelve lakhs.

I wanted to film Jackie's entry on some steps. We found a location in Dadar but the owner of the place asked for 5000 rupees. That was out of the question. So my assistant Yogesh and I drove around for hours looking for a location with steps. When we passed Antop Hill, I saw some steps leading to a water tank on the hill. I got very excited and thought I could shoot Jackie's entry there, and why not use the top of the water tank for Jackie's encounter with his rival? A setting like that would give the film scale, though in terms of logic it made no sense—why would Jackie and Tom Alter confront one another out in the open with the whole city around them?

Antop Hill was literally full of shit, because there was a slum nearby and people used the hillside for their morning activities. It stank. But it was the perfect spot. We got permission from the municipality, the BMC, and since nobody had shot there before, they gave it to me for 250 rupees a day. I changed the dialogue to justify the location. The gangster played by Tom Alter now says to Kishen [Jackie Shroff]: 'Meri basti se guzar kar mujh tak pahunchne waale tum pehle aadmi ho, Kishan. Aaj tak tumhaare baare mein sunaa tha . . . [You're the first man who has made it through my shanty town to find me, Kishen. Till today I had only heard about you . . .] 'Now you can see me too,' is Kishen's reply.

AJ: That was a far more exciting choice of location than the usual gangster den.

You used the city very well in *Parinda*. It's almost impossible to think of the film without Bombay—the cityscapes, the lights, the port. You even managed to shoot at the Gateway of India, didn't you?

VVC: That was crazy! I wanted to film the New Year's Eve celebrations at the Gateway, but to be honest we didn't have the money to pay for permissions. So we shot without permission, and to capture a variety of images showing crowds celebrating, we decided to film the scene over three years. During the first New Year's Eve, we took many shots of the thronging crowds without the main actors. I shot with the main actors in the second year.

When we went back to the Gateway of India for the last time, I had this idea to get a shot from the top of the Gateway looking down at the crowds. The effect I wanted was very ambitious. When Jackie hears of his brother's death he cries out in anger and pain—from his shot I wanted to cut to crowds reacting to his cry of anguish and then scattering in all directions.

To get to the top of the Gateway we had to climb many winding stairs behind a padlocked door. We were forced to break the old rusty padlock to get in. Though we had come fully prepared with a torch and everything, Vicky Chopra, my nephew, who had just arrived from Kashmir, lost that damn torch. So, Binod Pradhan, his camera attendant and I had to make our way up the stairs in total darkness.

The stairwell was full of pigeon shit and there were pigeons flying straight at us—it felt like Hitchcock's *The Birds*. We had no idea where and when those winding stairs would ever end. We must have climbed a thousand steps to get to the top. Binod Pradhan was a smoker, so thankfully he had a matchbox on him, so he kept striking a match to give us some light. Then we ran out of matches. It was pitch black. We couldn't see a f***ing thing.

Finally, we got to the top of the Gateway and took the shot from there. I wanted the crowd down below to part with a roar. Before we started our journey on those stairs, we had made friends with the cop on duty and gave him the necessary encouragement to help us out. We didn't have much film stock with us and had to be very careful about how much we could shoot. Binod started the camera, I waved a white handkerchief to attract the attention of the cop. There was no other way of communicating with him, so when he saw my signal, he kind of lathi-charged, or pretended to, and the crowd dispersed and we got a spectacular top shot!

AJ: Wonderful! I believe Nana Patekar helped you with crowd-control.

VVC: Nana Patekar was the guy who gave the 'necessary encouragement' to the cop. Marathi brotherhood came in handy there!

AJ: You've told me, but remind me what was the budget of *Parinda*?

VVC: Twelve lakhs. I didn't pay the actors; I couldn't pay many people, but they believed in me and worked for free— they knew if the film did well, I would pay them and I did.

AJ: And the film did well, didn't it?

VVC: We sold *Parinda* in all territories. My accountant told me I had a profit of forty-two lakhs. I was so delighted because I thought I could buy a home. I saw a three-bedroom flat for thirty lakhs on Zig-Zag Road in Bandra and made an offer on it. I was so excited. I gave the flat owner two lakhs in down payment and then my accountant tells me: 'I made a mistake, sir. We owe ten lakhs to the special effects team.'

A few days later, he comes to me with a sheepish look and says: 'I made another mistake, sir, we owe . . .' The same scenario went on for a week and soon enough my profit dwindled to twelve lakhs and we couldn't afford the apartment. I went back to the owner and said I didn't have the money to complete the deal. He asked me what had happened and I explained. He said: 'Normally we never return the down payment. But in your case, I know you're an honest guy. I've seen *Parinda*.'

He returned the two lakhs to me and then I started looking for a flat for around twelve lakhs. I found this house where we still live—Maria Cottage. At the time, it had two rooms, a kitchen and a terrace. Over the years, we've added many other rooms.

I must tell you about the guy who sold me Maria Cottage. I met him in his small shop near Mehboob Studio. He said he wanted eighteen lakhs.

Sir, I can't pay that. I can only pay twelve.
Nahin, itne mein toh hoga nahin. [No, that won't be enough.]

As I was getting up to leave, a tea vendor passed by. The owner asked if I wanted some tea. A free tea was always welcome so I said yes. While I was drinking the tea, this guy said: 'Nana Patekar ko dekha *Parinda* picture mein? Kamaal kiya! Yeh hota hain actor.' [Did you see Nana Patekar in *Parinda*? He was amazing. Now that's an actor for you.]

I believe the owner's name was Sadanand Raut. He asked me what I did for a living. I told him I made documentaries.

He said: 'Jaao picture dekho, tumko samajh mein aayega kya banaane ka. Vidhu Vinod Chopra banaaya picture.' [Go and see the movie. Then you'll understand how to make one. Vidhu Vinod Chopra has made the film.]

I put my tea glass down and told him I was Vidhu Vinod Chopra. Sadanand Raut looked at me stunned. When his excitement had settled, he asked me how I did this scene and that scene. I must have sat there for about half an hour or more. When I finally got up to go, he opened his drawer, took out some keys and gave them to me. I reminded him I couldn't afford to pay more than twelve lakhs for the cottage. He just smiled and said: 'I'll accept eleven lakhs. Because it's you.'

And he threw in the terrace for Rs 25,000. *Parinda* got me my first home.

AJ: I heard *Parinda* would have made much more money if it had another ending, but you refused to change the ending.

VVC: I might've made more money, but the film would have felt false to me. If Anil and Madhuri had lived and Jackie was killed, it was the usual clichéd story ending. Most importantly, such an ending was the opposite of the premise of the film—that violence begets violence.

Parinda had the right ending—Jackie had to be seen lighting the funeral pyres of Anil Kapoor and Madhuri Dixit.

AJ: Killing off the hero and heroine must have been a tough call.

VVC: Yes, it was. The distributor in Punjab, Gurdeep Singh, called me from Jalandhar near the end of the first show, first day and said: 'When Anil and Madhuri are murdered at the end of the film, people are clapping and saying what a wonderful dream sequence! But I know you've really killed them and when the audience realize they're really dead, they're going to tear the seats and kill me. Please do some editing tonight and let them live. Kill Jackie instead.'

Abhijat, he said all this in Punjabi and it sounded damn funny.

AJ: Didn't people say *Parinda* would be your last film?

VVC: They did! Because they thought no one would accept the ending.

AJ: Tell me how you worked with your team. Binod Pradhan, the DOP. Renu, who edited your films. They were your closest allies.

VVC: In those days, and it's true even now, before we started filming, my team and I discuss the look of the film and refer to many things. Back then it was Binod Pradhan and I who studied the work of great painters like Van Gogh and Renoir to try and find the one painting that might determine the look the film could have.

It used to be very difficult to watch international cinema in India. It was not as easy as today—you have satellite television, the streaming channels and DVDs, etc. The only way we could see a European movie was if it happened to be playing in a theatre. The kind of references you have today—like seeing a hundred ways of lighting a scene or how to design sound effects—none of this was available to us. That's why Binod and I referred to paintings.

There was another problem. If you had a love scene in a Hindi film, you were asking for trouble. Sex on the screen was taboo for decades and a love scene provoked catcalls, whistles and vulgar comments from the audience, plus the censors would most likely kill it and ask you to cut the scene. It was a big challenge for us to find ways of including a love scene where audiences would not whistle or the censors not ask for cuts.

I was married to Shabnam Sukhdev at the time, so she, Binod Pradhan and I took stills of her neck, waist and arms, etc. I showed the stills to Madhuri Dixit and said this is how we'll film you—the camera will glide over you and no detail will be shown. We storyboarded the scene using these stills. Storyboarding was hardly practised in India then.

When we finally shot the scene, we used dim lighting and the lovemaking was suggestive, not vulgar. When *Parinda* was released, no one whistled during the love scene, because they were totally involved with the characters. They weren't seeing them as stars making love. That was a big relief.

AJ: Many young directors consider *Parinda* a great film because of your innovative approach. Unbelievable things happen in the last forty minutes. This was in the late 1980s; we had not seen editing like that before. How did you conceive those scenes?

VVC: Shots like the uncapping of the bottle or the shot of pigeons flying into the sky were fun to conceive. I worked a lot with images and sounds. I knew exactly how certain scenes should look.

For example, I deliberately had a jhoola in Nana's house. And the bed on the ship where Anil and Madhuri spend their wedding night had also to be placed on a wide jhoola. My art directors, Nitish Roy and Nitin Desai, said it was not realistic because when the ship moved the jhoola was bound to hit the side of the ship. I said: 'I don't give a shit about reality. I want realism. There's a big difference between the two. I want the nuptial bed on that swing. So, when Anil and Madhuri are shot, the chains of the swing snap and the swing is left dangling. Then I'll cut to Nana's room, we'll see the chains of his jhoola from Jackie's point of view as he enters. The two events must be linked visually in Jackie's mind.'

AJ: It worked very well. Then there's the famous pigeons flying scene.

VVC: When I first came to Bombay, we would take the train from Dadar to Pune. One day I was walking from the station looking for a bus when I saw this Kabutar Khana. My first reaction was—my God, this is really cinematic. Pigeons were everywhere—on the ground and in the air! It was completely mad to think we could shoot there because there was so much traffic on all the roads around the Kabutar Khana. But we managed to get permission. When we were shouting at the shopkeepers to shut their shops, the rumour went around that I was PM Rajiv Gandhi's relative. Everybody thought I had to be, otherwise there was no way in hell I would have got permission to close the shops in the middle of the day. When I heard about this wild rumour, I told my production team: 'Don't say a word till we get out of here. Long live the rumour!'

AJ: Wasn't there talk that you wanted to cast a leading female star in *Parinda?*

VVC: Yeah! My assistant Janak Toprani went to see her. I don't want to name her but it was a well-known fact that her mother insisted on listening to the script narrations before her daughter signed a film. Janak came back to me and said her mother had given us time for a narration the next day and she was going to hear the script! I asked Janak to get her on the line.

Yes, Mr Chopra, come tomorrow at 11 a.m. and narrate the story.
Mr Chopra can't come tomorrow, he's in Kashmir.
Then who are you? Aren't you Mr Chopra?
I'm Vinod.
Then who is Mr Chopra?
My father. He's in Kashmir. He'll have to come to Bombay to narrate the script to you.
Why does he have to come?
The director's father must narrate the story to the heroine's mother and once the mother and father are happy, we children will take it forward.

She was so pissed off with me that she banged the phone down. Maybe five years after that call, I met her somewhere and I'll never forget the look she gave me. [*both laugh*] But that's how I was, Abhijat. Righteous to the extent of madness!

AJ: I remember your man Friday, Rattan, changed his opinion about you when he saw you filming *Parinda.*

VVC: Rattan was from Nepal. On the first day of the shoot, we were filming Jackie at the airport where he was supposed to receive his brother Anil from America. Rattan was driving my van that day and he sat watching me work. I had to run up and down five flights of stairs all morning giving instructions to the cast and crew. It was exhausting. Remember there were no walkie-talkies back then.

Later that evening, Rattan came into my room and asked if he could massage my feet. I said no. Usually that was enough to send him away. But he didn't budge. A few minutes later, he asked if I wanted tea. I asked him to leave me alone. Rattan then insisted he owed me an apology. I thought he had stolen something. I was preoccupied with writing the scene for the next day's shoot and explained I was busy, but he wanted to talk to me so badly that I had to hear him out.

He started off by asking if he could call me 'Vidhu Chacha'. Then he said: 'I'm very sorry. For years I've told all the servants in the building that my boss is a faltu [useless] bugger. He just keeps writing something and sleeps all afternoon. And it's his brother who sends him money. Today I realized who you really are.' [*both laugh*]

I have so many memories connected to *Parinda*. One day I saw a sardar just lying on the street. He had met with an accident. No one was helping him. I suppose bystanders don't usually help accident victims in Indian cities because they fear the cops will implicate them and they'll end up in trouble themselves. It happens so often. That's why strangers are reluctant to help.

I helped the sardar get into my car and took him to the emergency room at Nanavati Hospital. One of the doctors there saw me and asked me not to leave. I thought he was going to call the police. Then a group of doctors came looking very intense. They asked me:

Did Anna set his wife on fire?
Why ask me?
We have a 500-rupee bet. My friend says he did and I bet he didn't.
I don't know if Anna burned his wife.
What do you mean you don't know? You made the film!
In the film, Anna says he did not kill her. But how do I know if he's telling the truth or not.

The doctors looked totally baffled as I walked away. By the way, the sardar recovered well. He's a carpenter and later he became a friend.

AJ: You've met many people in your life. Was there anyone who influenced the way you looked at life?

VVC: Back in 1973, Ramanand Sagar produced a film called *Jalte Badan*. It was around the time when I was a first-year student at the FTII. He had organized a screening of his film at Natraj Studio and I watched the movie with his distributors, family and friends. When the film was over, everyone started praising it. They raved about it. I was quiet and said nothing.

When it was time to leave Natraj, I decided to take the bus back to Pune. Suddenly Praji—that's what we called Ramanand Sagar—said:

Come with me.
No, thank you, Praji. I'll catch the bus.
Get in. I'll drop you at the bus stop.

I had no option but to get into his car. He had a white Impala and his driver's name was John. Now in this sprawling Impala, there's only him and me sitting at the back. I'm in full panic—why is he taking me with him? The moment we left the gates of the studio, he asked:

Vidhu, kaisi lagi tenu film? [What do you think of the movie?]
My opinion is irrelevant. Everybody loves it. Your distributors love it.
Yes. I know what they think. I'm asking you what you think.

I tried to be a little diplomatic but I am not a diplomatic man by nature and told him it was rubbish. I added it was sad that a man like him who was capable of making much better films, and *had* made much better films, was making nonsense like this just because it might make money. As I finished talking, we arrived at the 81 bus stop on S.V. Road and I asked John to let me out. As I was getting out of his Impala, Ramanand Sagar said: 'I hear you. But you're a pauper, so you're talking big. The day you become a big man and travel in an Impala like me, instead of taking the bus, we'll talk.'

That's all he said. And—zoom—he drove off and I just stood at the bus stop for a long time, letting the enormity of what he had just said sink in.

Years later when Ramanand Sagar was unwell, I went to see him. By then I owned more than one expensive car. I wanted to express my gratitude to him for having said what he had that day: 'Praji, there was something that happened thirty or forty years ago, and I want to tell you how that incident changed my life. I'm so grateful you said what you did. After the screening of *Jalte Badan*, we were driving in your car and you told me . . .'

He stopped me mid-sentence and said: 'I remember . . .' Then he repeated the exact words that he said to me in his Impala that evening. He finished by adding: 'Vinod, I am so proud of you.'

For me the conversation we had in his car was a life-changing moment, but what shocked me was that he had remembered it so vividly and after decades. I thought it was nothing to him but somehow it affected him too.

Ramanand Sagar sent me a very touching letter after I won a National Award for *Parineeta*. I still have it. He said

I was the jewel of our family. Perhaps in the beginning he felt some sort of anger towards me—because I was doing things my way. I had taken a different path from his, what with going to film school, etc. But when I became successful and he saw *Parinda* and the other movies I made, like *1942: A Love Story*, I think he changed his mind about me. He became affectionate and loving, his attitude towards me had changed.

AJ: You did take another path from his. Instead of joining the film industry directly, you went to film school.

There are still many hundreds of hopefuls who apply each year to the FTII. Was it difficult for you to get admission?

VVC: I was interviewed by a panel that included the great writer Krishan Chander and the great director Hrishikesh Mukherjee. Krishan Chander had written a film for Ramanand Sagar and they were close friends because they were both writers, though he didn't know that Ramanand Sagar and I were related. At the selection interview, they asked:

> You got a first-class degree in economics. You were hoping to go to Cambridge for a PhD, so what brings you here?
> *Because I'm stupid.*

They laughed and Hrishida said:

Are you suggesting everybody who comes to the film institute is stupid?

No. But if they had a choice between a PhD from Cambridge and a diploma in cinema from Pune, and they opt for the diploma, of course they're being stupid.

May I ask you why you're being stupid?

I answered with great arrogance: 'I'm letting my childhood passion overrule my rational senses.' Then Krishan Chander asked me if I had ever written any short stories. I proceeded to tell the panel a story from the Mahabharata. A story that my father had narrated to me. It was about a legendary writer whose guru instructs him to write a story every day to better his art.

A writer once lived in a guru's ashram and each day he went to the guru with a new story. Showing no expression, the guru tore up the story and asked the writer to write another. This went on for fourteen long years. At the end of fourteen years when the guru was about to tear up yet another story, the writer fell at his feet and implored him not to destroy this one. The writer had tears in his eyes and soon the guru too started weeping. The writer was surprised to see his guru cry. A few minutes passed and then the guru spoke: 'Take your story and leave my ashram. You do not need me any more. You've been way ahead of me for some time. As I read your stories, year after year, I was waiting for you to stop me from destroying your fine writing.'

I ended the story by saying I longed for the day when I could not tear up my stories. That was the end of the FTII interview. I was in!

AJ: What an interview!

VVC: Yes! Later that day I was in the canteen having tea with two fellow students, Ashok Ahuja and Saeed Mirza—they were selected too. Krishan Chander's son, Munir, came into the canteen and asked who among us was Ramanand Sagar's brother. Through the canteen window I could see Krishan Chander waiting in a white Ambassador. The last thing I wanted was to be selected because I was Ramanand Sagar's brother. I looked at Ashok Ahuja and said:

> Oh shit! Are you Ramanand Sagar's brother?
> *How can I be his brother? My name is Ashok Ahuja.*
> I'm Vinod Chopra. Is there anyone with the surname Sagar here?

Most people did not know Ramanand Sagar's real name was Ramanand Chopra. Saeed Mirza smiled and said: 'Hell, no! I'm a Muslim. I can't be his brother.'

We all had a good laugh and Munir left the canteen to join his father and they drove away. Later that evening, I went to see Hrishida. He was staying at a hotel near the Deccan Gymkhana and I asked him if I had been selected because of my connection to Ramanand Sagar. He said he wasn't even aware we were related until I had mentioned it.

To this day I'm still not sure whether he was telling me the truth, but I remember saying: 'Either you're telling me the truth or you are a fine actor, Hrishida. But thank you very much for convincing me to study at the FTII.'

AJ: How was your relationship with Hrishikesh Mukherjee?

VVC: He was always supportive. I once filmed a song in a single shot and he liked that. He knew I was always trying to push the envelope.

I remember he watched *Murder at Monkey Hill* at Mohan Studio on an editing device called the Moviola. At the end of the film, some frames of celluloid looked as if they were being ripped. Hrishida stopped the Moviola immediately, thinking it was damaging my film. I explained the ripping was a planned special effect. He said: 'I know, I know.' Hrishida was a brilliant film editor but I knew I had him fooled! I was so thrilled.

AJ: You went to meet him in his last days. I believe he told you he should have pursued chemistry instead of becoming a film-maker.

VVC: Yes. It was a sad moment. I think Raju Hirani was with me. Hrishida was unwell and looked very weak. He said:

> I have one regret. I should have become a chemist. I
> should not have made films.
> *What are you saying, Dada?*
> I have never made a great film.

It was sad and yet instructive. He was a great film-maker and he made some very good films, but in his head he could have done better. What I learnt that day was to always strive for excellence. Strive for your best; your second best won't do—even if your second best is good enough for the world.

AJ: Did the same thought ever cross your mind—that you could have done better?

VVC: When I made *Parinda*, *1942: A Love Story*, *Eklavya*, *Broken Horses*, *Munna Bhai* or *3 Idiots*, I believed it was the best I could do as a director or producer. Sometimes I succeeded, sometimes I failed. When I die, I'll know I tried my best every time, though in some cases, like *Broken Horses*, I believe my best was not good enough. Then again, in *Shikara*, I believe my best was good enough.

AJ: You told me about the time when Mr R.K. Laxman came to the FTII and gave some sound advice to you students.

VVC: He talked to us very briefly. His words showed me a way in which I could lead my life. What he said was full of insight: 'Good cinema makes bad money and bad cinema makes good money. I want you guys to make good cinema that makes good money.'

AJ: The brilliant Ritwik Ghatak taught at the FTII before your time. But I remember you saying he sometimes visited when you were there. I believe you had to take him to the hospital once. You said he was going to die that day. Is that right?

VVC: Yes, absolutely. Some Bengali students and I took him to the Ruby Hall Clinic in Pune. We were very worried that he was going to die, uncared for.

Ghatak was drinking heavily and his liver had given up. Because none of us had any money, he had to be admitted into a general ward. They treated him very badly. For them, Ghatak was just an old drunkard. I wept that day and thought: 'My God! Here, in this general ward is Ritwik Ghatak, probably one of the greatest film-makers India has ever seen, and he's dying. If it had been a top Bollywood director, he would not be lying in a general ward but in a five-star luxury hospital.'

It was a sad realization but it made me think—I didn't want to be a highly successful mediocre Hindi film director; nor did I want to die like Ritwik Ghatak. But what were my choices? How could I make the cinema I found fulfilling yet not end up dying in a general ward with no one to care for me?

I think that incident had a great impact on me. Today I'm successful and happy to be where I am. I don't think I've made films I'm ashamed of and I don't think I'm going to die in a general ward.

AJ: Did Ritwik Ghatak's cinema influence you?

VVC: I'm still amazed by the way he used sound in his movies—it's just stunning. Think of *Meghe Dhaka Tara* or *Ajantrik.* He was mad in his own way but he was a great teacher and a great film-maker. When he'd come to the FTII, he talked about everything under the sun, from films to Shakespeare.

We had a crazy relationship; I mean the little I had to do with him. And of course we sometimes sat together under the famous Wisdom Tree. He spoke to me in Bengali and though I did not understand Bengali very well, he refused to speak to me in English. He said I was not a Kashmiri but a Bengali.

Did you know my name 'Vidhu Vinod' came from Ritwik Ghatak? Yes! My birth name is Vinod Kumar Chopra. My family called me Vidhu. One day Ghatak declared: 'What kind of name is that? Binod Kumar Chopra? You should have a majestic and powerful name like mine—Ritwik Ghatak!'

So he suggested I call myself 'Bidhu Binod Chopra'. He pronounced my name as Bengalis do and it was on that day he planted the idea in my mind to start using the name inspired by him.

AJ: You've met some wonderful people. There was also Mr Bachchan for whom you even wrote a script in the early days. Am I right?

VVC: Yes, that was the script I was writing when Mr Shastri gave me the job at Doordarshan. It was called *Prashant*, but was shelved when I decided to make shorts for DD. I still have the script somewhere.

When I started writing *Prashant*, I was very poor so I asked Amitabh if he could give me 2000 rupees a month so I could continue writing. He looked very confused and said: 'You know, you're a strange guy. You're supposed to pay *me*. You're the one who wants to sign me for a film.'

I explained I had no money and needed 2000 rupees. The next day I went back to see him. I was sure he would give me the money but instead he said: 'I can't. Because people in the industry will say I've started paying people to write for me.'

Whatever his reason, as far as I was concerned, I didn't get the 2000. I had no money at all. That's the time I won 4000 bucks and the National Award for my first short film. The next time I met him I told him I didn't want his money any more and added: 'I've bought a ceiling fan and got a phone connection with my prize money. You can reach me at any time now. The phone is right next to my bed.' And I proudly gave him my number.

There was no ceiling fan in the one room that Renu and I were renting as paying guests and in the summer it was sheer hell. So it was wonderful to finally have a fan whirling over our bed through the night. Thanks to that fan, I slept like a baby.

In the early days, I think Amitabh found me amusing. While I was still writing the script of *Prashant*, I designed the poster and showed it to him. He said:

How come you're designing a poster? Doesn't one write the film first?
No, I design the poster first. That shows the direction I want my screenplay to take.

I'm sure Amit—that's what I had started calling him— thought I was completely crazy to walk away from the chance of working with him. In early 2020, I happened to see for the first time ever that Renu Saluja had written 'I love you' on the bottom of the piece of paper where I had noted my decision to drop the idea of making *Prashant*. Anyway, that's how Mr Bachchan and I parted . . . till *Eklavya* happened many years later.

AJ: There was a kind of friendship between the two of you. Didn't you once show Mr Bachchan *Red Beard* by Kurosawa? If I remember correctly, that was a difficult phase in his life.

VVC: Very difficult. There was a magazine on his table, I don't remember which one, but the cover had these words written over an image of Amitabh: 'The end of an icon.'

Six months later, I went to see him and the magazine was still sitting on top of his files. I asked him: 'Why are you torturing yourself? Why do you keep this here? Must you look at it every morning?' He said nothing and just smiled. He's a very interesting man and I'm sure deep down he was thinking: 'I'll show them all.'

And he did. He came out of that low phase and we all know where Amitabh Bachchan is today.

AJ: So you finally got to work with him in *Eklavya*. I am curious to know why you used two cameras to shoot the film. Was it the first time you had shot with two cameras?

VVC: Yes. The primary reason was financial. I had to finish the film quickly and this way I saved time. It's a nice and efficient way of working.

The filming was supposed to be completed in thirty-seven days and we finished it in about thirty-four. My line producer said: 'This is the first time not a rupee of the contingency budget has been used. Not a single rupee.'

AJ: Wasn't Amitabh Bachchan supposed to act in *Mission Kashmir,* but the dates didn't work out? That's when he was making *Kaun Banega Crorepati*. Right?

VVC: *Kaun Banega Crorepati* was a massive success. I called to congratulate him and he thanked me very formally. Then I asked: 'By the way, have you got rid of that magazine from your desk?' He started laughing and said he had.

His greatest contribution to my life was the question he asked me at Natraj Studio: 'When do we work together?' I will always owe him because his words gave me so much confidence.

AJ: I think Mr Bachchan has tremendous affection for you. You guys had that great evening at your place when he came by.

VVC: One evening he called me and asked where I was at that moment. I told him I'm always at home. So he came over to Maria Cottage and recited his father's poems to us. I asked him what made him call me out of the blue. His answer surprised me: 'Iss sheher mein main kahaan jaunga Babu-ji ki poetry recite karne?' [Where in this city can I go to recite Babu-ji's poetry?] I was very touched.

AJ: At one point, you said you did not want to make *Eklavya* without Mr Bachchan.

VVC: Without him, the film would have made no sense because the main character is inspired by him.

One day we were travelling in his car and his words inspired me to write the story of *Eklavya*. I don't remember exactly what he said, but it was on the lines of: 'You're a blessed man, Vinod. Whatever you have in your heart, you can spill it out, just like that.' He tapped his chest and continued:

> Everything stays inside here! All bottled up. It doesn't come out. It all stays inside.
> *Are you crazy? You're Amitabh Bachchan. You can take it out.*
> Nahin nikaal sakta, yaar. [No, I can't let it out, my friend.]

His words stayed with me and later found shape in the development of the lead character in *Eklavya*. Eklavya is the biological father of the prince, played by Saif Ali Khan, but he does not tell his own son that he's his father. His sense of duty, manhood, the burden of centuries, everything weighs him down.

I remember the shooting very well. It was a long schedule in Rajasthan and Amitabh arrived with just a few bags. When I looked puzzled, he explained: 'Jaya hasn't sent all my things. She's sure I'll be back in a week and believes we cannot work together and there's no way I will stay longer than a week.' We laughed about it but what followed was exactly as his wife had predicted.

Amitabh was late on day one of the shoot. And because he was late we missed the light we wanted. I went to his van and said: 'Our shooting schedule is for forty-one days so we have to like one another for forty-one days. After that it doesn't matter if we don't get on.'

In his deep baritone voice, he said:

I don't know, Vinod, what gives you the impression I don't care for you? I really like . . .
I am not talking about you, Amit. I'm talking about me.
Why?
You can't come bloody late on the set, yaar! I missed my magic hour light. I can't take the shot now. We have to reschedule—the light has gone. So I don't like you at this moment, Amit.

He was a little late the next day too, but not by too much. The third shoot day was critical. The crane shot was ready, the sun was setting and my light was disappearing fast. I shouted to my assistant Tanya: 'Ask Mr Bachchan's assistant Praveen Jain to come here at once. We're going to lose the light. I want Amit here now!'

Tanya came back and said Praveen had refused to come. I completely lost it. I could see my light disappearing. I knew I had lost the shot. I came down from the crane and saw Sanjay Dutt standing there. I told him: 'Put on Eklavya's costume, you're not playing Pannalal Chohar but Eklavya. End of story. I'm done with Bachchan.'

Pradeep Sarkar was there and he tried to stop me. Anupama was there too, but she stayed out of it. I was furious. As I walked down the steps to his room, I saw Praveen, I shouted at him: 'Why didn't you come when I called you?'

Amitabh could hear me from inside his dressing room but that didn't bother me. I carried on shouting at Praveen: 'You don't work for him, Praveen. You take your daily allowance from me. Right now you're not his employee, you're my employee. And if you're paid by me, you bloody well come when I ask you to.'

Praveen tried to argue and I got even madder and told my production guys: 'Khadda khodo, isko main yahin dabaa deta hoon.' [Dig a hole, I'm going to bury this fellow right here.] I then shouted for my line producer:

How much money have we spent so far?
Close to a crore.
Write it off.

Amitabh could hear every word I was saying. I told Praveen to get Eklavya's costume and beard and give them to Sanjay Dutt. Everyone figured that was the end and Mr Bachchan was bound to come out and say: 'Damn you! You're crazy. Jaya warned me. I'm going.'

Finally, Amitabh came out of his room and walked towards us; everybody went silent. He had his costume and beard on. He went straight over to Anupama and asked: 'How do you live with this madman? He's crazy!'

She started laughing and Amitabh started laughing. I started laughing and then the whole crew was laughing. He said: 'Do you know how difficult it is to put this beard on? The guys who stick it on my face really stink and they're all over me and it takes hours. If I showed up on set and the beard was not right, you would scream.'

The next day, I told the make-up guys to have a bath with Dettol and wear white hospital gowns. At four the next morning, I heard Bachchan shouting. The make-up guys had walked in with face masks and smelling of Dettol. Amit told me later his make-up room felt just like a hospital. In my half-sleep state, I then heard his security jeep siren wailing away in the distance. My assistant came running to me and woke me up.

Sir, Mr Bachchan has gone to the location.
But the call sheet is for 6 a.m. It's only 5.
Sir, I know. But he's gone.

I had two options: I could head to the location or go back to sleep. As I had hardly slept for days, I decided to go back to sleep for another hour. At 6 a.m., I left for the location and saw Mr Bachchan. He had this habit of stacking five plastic chairs, one on top of the other, and there he was sitting on that raised stack. I smiled and asked him why he had come to the location so early. He replied: 'I don't like to be shouted at, sir. I was playing it safe.' What else could I do but quietly walk away? He's like a kid, yaar! [*both laugh*] 5 a.m. he goes and sits in the middle of nowhere.

When the shoot was over, he wanted a private plane to take him back to Bombay. I had to refuse because the budget couldn't be stretched. He chartered a plane from

Jodhpur and paid for it himself, and Anu and I hitched a plane ride with him. I hadn't paid Amitabh for the film, yet he gave me one of my first private plane rides!

AJ: You showed me a witty exchange of text messages between you both when he was in Agra. You were thinking of an actor to cast in the role of Rana and he texted back suggesting Naseeruddin Shah's name. You replied:

> But Naseer can be crazy.
> *That's what I hear about you.*
> Without madness cinema is not possible.
> *I'm up for that kind of madness.*
> Don't say that too loudly, Amit. You're in Agra!

AJ: You mentioned Agra because it's well known there's a famous mental asylum there! I found that story very funny.

You put everything into *Eklavya*. I'm thinking of three sequences that you were not happy with, so you changed them. The killing of the Jimmy Sheirgill character . . .

VVC: When I was working with Bejoy Nambiar on *Wazir*, he asked about the scene you just mentioned and how I managed to hold the shot for two minutes—you see nothing but a black screen.

AJ: You described it as 'cinema without visuals'.

VVC: [*smiles*] We had an intricate sound design that made the moment quite dramatic.

AJ: What was your reference for this scene?

VVC: The Hollywood film *Wait Until Dark*. They used darkness very well. The protagonist, played by Audrey Hepburn, is blind and to escape the man who is out to murder her, she unscrews all the bulbs in her flat so there's total darkness. When the man enters her room that night, he cannot see a thing. He fumbles around for a few minutes and during this time we're watching a black screen. Then she hears the fridge door open and there's the hum of the fridge, and she knows the fridge bulb will light the room. Now how will she escape the murderer?

Having seen the black-screen shot in *Eklavya*, I think the columnist and author Shobhaa De wrote something like this about me: 'Either he has real balls or he's nuts. Or both.'

Abhijat, what was the second scene you were thinking of?

AJ: The bell scene.

VVC: I am never very comfortable with digital effects because you have to rely on others. It's a pain in the butt—you conceive something that you cannot execute. That bell scene drove me up the wall. And the third sequence?

AJ: The camel sequence.

VVC: Oh, that was tough! A train is approaching and some camels grazing near the tracks were supposed to move away—at least that was the whole idea! But I discovered camels don't budge. They are the worst animals you could possibly hope to direct. [*both laugh*]

When I was sweating under that hot Rajasthani sun, I thought of David Lean who said something like, 'You can't direct a camel.' He was so right. Camels don't take instructions! It was quite a task getting them to run in the opposite direction as the train approached. You can see that shot in the film—the car, the train, the camels. There's nothing digitally created in the scene, it's all real.

AJ: You told me shooting *Eklavya* was one of the most challenging shoots of your entire life, especially as you had to film in temperatures running up to 50 degrees in Rajasthan.

VVC: Oh my god, was it hot! You can't even imagine how hot. It was ridiculous. You couldn't shoot in the afternoons. We filmed in the mornings and by twelve we had to stop for three hours. At three or four, we went back to work. It was burning hot and even the rubber lining on our equipment had started melting.

AJ: Didn't Boman Irani faint during the shoot?

VVC: Yes. I thought he was acting but he had really fainted. It was so hot. Amit started shouting for us to get water for him.

Remember the bullet that zips by Boman? We could not fake that—it would not have worked because CGI was so terrible in those days. With Boman in the frame, my stunt man took a gun and shot through the glass and BOOM! I thought Boman was very brave. He didn't run away.

AJ: In the scene when King Jaywardhan (Boman Irani) dies, you thought you should have something to punctuate the ending of the scene. That's when you had a solitary camel pass as the king lies dying in Eklavya's arms.

VVC: I really like that shot. They are holding one another—the sun is setting and a camel walks past in the foreground with the soft sound of the bell jangling around its neck.

AJ: It was a serene moment while everything before it was violent; the speeding train, the camels, Rana crying out, Eklavya's desperation—big sounds.

Another death scene I found impressive was Jackie dying in *Eklavya*.

VVC: Actually, Jackie had to stand a foot or two away from a fast-moving train. I had dust and wind blowing all around him. In one of his interviews, Jackie said: 'Oh shit! If any of these bogies come a few inches closer to me, I'll be crushed to death.'

He could've easily been hit by the train. That was a tough shot. But I must say all the actors stood by me despite the difficult shooting conditions. The kind of commitment Amit, Jackie, Sanjay Dutt, Saif Ali Khan, Vidya Balan and my team showed was quite amazing.

AJ: You went to a lot of trouble to get the details right in *Eklavya*.

VVC: I don't know if these things are appreciated. At the time the film released, in 2007, cinema literacy in India was lower than it is now.

I believe to appreciate a good painting you have to know a little about the art of painting. To read Hindi or any language, you need to know the language. In the same way, to enjoy a film you have to know a bit about cinema language, otherwise you cannot appreciate it fully. But the truth is we must do whatever makes us happy, whatever gives us a high as film-makers. If the audiences notice the details, it's wonderful, if not, that's fine too, because the scene will make us happy every time we see it. And that's all that matters.

AJ: I recall a very funny incident during the shoot of *Eklavya* in Rajasthan. We used to sleep in tents and one night . . . remember, sir?

VVC: I remember! One night, Shantanu Moitra, Swanand Kirkire and you were all excited about an idea you had and were keen to share it with me. The other guys did not want to disturb me but you entered my tent and woke me up saying you had this brilliant idea.

AJ: Yes, sir! You looked at me and said: 'I've opened one eye, if your idea is any good, I'll open the other!'

But when I told you what the idea was, you turned to one side, saying: 'It's bullshit!'

You shut your eyes and went straight back to sleep. As I made my way out of the tent, I heard you snoring again! [*both laugh*]

I think at one point, you were looking at international distribution when you were making *Eklavya*. Did you think it could be your calling card in America? I think your sister Shelly, in fact, gave a DVD of the film to Jeff Berg.

VVC: Yes. Jeff Berg was the chairman and CEO of ICM. He didn't know me at all, but when he saw the film, he emailed me. I thought it was some prank. The mail said he represented Bernardo Bertolucci and Roman Polanski, and having seen my work, he felt it was of the same calibre and asked to represent me. And that's how I got representation in Hollywood.

Nicolas Cage saw *Eklavya* many times and said it made him cry every time. I asked him jokingly: 'What were you smoking?' [*both laugh*]

The film was a calling card for me. When I finally made *Broken Horses*, it was *Eklavya* that got everybody on board.

AJ: As the film wasn't well received in India, it must have been heartening to have a good reaction in Hollywood. What was the *Los Angeles Times* story you once told me?

VVC: I was having a shower when a friend from Los Angeles called to say the *LA Times* critic had described *Eklavya* as a lost work of David Lean's. I thought this guy was fooling me and said: 'Come on! It's early morning, go to sleep.

Don't bullshit me.' My friend sent me the link and it made me feel on top of the world when I read it. [*both smile*]

I don't think I was disappointed about how *Eklavya* was received in India. I was disappointed when *Parinda* did not do as well as I thought it would have, but I was pretty certain about *Eklavya*'s fate here. I knew it wouldn't do well. But that was okay. It did not stop me from making the movie I wanted to.

I knew full well there was no way in hell that *Shikara* would do the business of, let's say, a *Munna Bhai*. But some films have to be made and someone like me needs to make them because money is not what drives me. I am blessed in that way.

Lage Raho Munna Bhai and *Eklavya* released in the same year. I remember telling my chartered accountant, Anil Sekhri, that one film will make money and the other one will lose money. The guy looked at me.

Why are you making movies that lose money?
You're a chartered accountant. It's something I'll never be able to explain to you.

AJ: I remember you once said: 'If you make a film to please others without liking it yourself, and if others don't like it either, there will be nobody in the world who will like your film. Especially as you weren't convinced that you like it either.'

VVC: Absolutely. That's what I still believe. I made *Broken Horses* and it didn't do well. Am I disappointed? No, I'm not. It's probably not one of my best films but I loved the fact that I went out of my comfort zone and tried something new. It would've been wonderful if the movie had done well. But I am not disappointed as an artist. Could I have done better? Maybe yes. But I did my best. And if my best was not good enough, it's okay.

I must tell you a story. Zuni, Agni and I were going to the airport and we saw a large hoarding; it was an ad for Nike and it said something about brilliance. I said excellence is more important. So my kids asked me to explain the difference between excellence and brilliance and I said: 'Brilliance is when other people appreciate your work and think you're brilliant. But excellence has nothing to do with other people. Excellence is something you strive for within yourself. Only you know when you have excelled. Only you know . . .'

I was speaking so passionately and excitedly that Zuni, who was very young at the time, calmed me down saying: 'Dad, don't get so agitated. It's just a hoarding!'

She was right. It was just a hoarding! But for me it was a life lesson.

AJ: You've shied away from making ads, but almost thirty years ago you made the hugely successful Pepsi ad and earned much more than you did in *Parinda*.

VVC: That's true! My profit was over fifty lakhs for that one-minute advert. I got a crore or something ridiculous for the production. And that was almost thirty years ago. So just imagine what the equivalent of a crore would be in today's money.

Actually, I could not believe the scale of that shoot! I walked into Mehboob Studio and saw thousands of extras waiting for me to direct them. The first thing I had to do was rush to the loo! I ran to Juhi Chawla's make-up room, because I didn't have a make-up room of my own and I used her toilet. I was terrified.

Pepsi was not available in India at the time. The ad was being made to announce its arrival. I wanted all the extras to drink from a bottle of Pepsi, so we had to buy a whole lot of kala khatta—the purplish syrup made from jamuns used to make ice candies, etc.—and we mixed it with soda. We poured it into empty Pepsi bottles and to motivate the actors and extras, I shouted over the mic: 'You're the first guys in India to taste Pepsi. Open the bottle, take a sip and say, "Aahh!" Just think, you're the first lucky ones in India to taste Pepsi!'

AJ: I liked the top shot of the crowd saying 'aah' as they sipped their drink. How did you do that shot?

VVC: It must have been the first time anyone had dared to put a trolley on those very high catwalks in Mehboob Studio . . .

AJ: That was very dangerous!

VVC: Absolutely! I joined two catwalks and put a trolley on them. Binod Pradhan and I were hanging in the middle and we could have easily hit the ground. The trolley was pushed along the catwalk. That's how we took the top shot.

Unfortunately, I tripped on the set and fell. When I had my little accident, the first thing I told the Pepsi guy who was there was: 'Shit, man! It would be terrible if I died on this set because if I had died making *Parinda*, at least they'd say he died with dignity. It would be such a disgrace if I died making an ad.' [*both laugh*]

AJ: The whole Pepsi team loved the ad and as a result you were invited to America to meet Alan Pottasch, the Pespi vice-chairman and creative head. Was it fun meeting him?

VVC: Yes, yaar! I flew to New York and they sent me a limo to take me from the hotel to the Pepsi headquarters. When I met Mr Pottasch's secretary, she said my appointment was at 12.15 p.m. and politely informed me that Mr Pottasch's next meeting was at 12.30 p.m. I got really pissed off. I was young and hot-blooded and thought: This guy calls me all the way from India for a fifteen-minute meeting?

Being the cocky fellow I was, I assumed he was going to take me out for lunch; instead, I was given fifteen minutes. When I entered Alan's office, he was watching my ad on a big TV monitor. He stopped the tape on a certain shot and asked me how I had done it. I explained to him that I had placed the camera in front of a black stage that was revolving from left to right and got Juhi Chawla to dance right to left. In the background, there was a neon Pepsi sign and that was moving in the opposite direction too. So things and people were criss-crossing each other in the same shot. We're talking about an era way before CGI.

Alan Pottasch was pretty impressed. He explained that he had called me to America to ask if I was interested in introducing Pepsi in the Gulf. He started by saying:

I know there was some issue with your payment. You were paid Indian rates, but for the Gulf, I'll pay you four times that amount. You'll get what I pay my American directors.
That gives me all the more reason to say no.
What do you mean?
Do you know why I'm saying no? It's because I made too much money making the Pepsi ad.
What do you mean 'too much money'?
In Parinda, *I made twelve lakhs. I made over fifty lakhs making the ad. Will I ever make a* Parinda *again if I made another Pepsi advert?*
Of course, you will. You're strong-willed.
I'm not that strong-willed. If I say yes to so much money, I'll stop making films like Parinda. *That's why I'm saying no.*
Can I try convincing you?
Sir, you have less than a minute to convince me because your next meeting is at 12.30.

He smiled, picked up the phone and called his secretary: 'Cancel my 12.30. I'm having lunch with Mr Chopra.'

Not only did he invite me to lunch, but that evening he took me in his private plane to a nearby town. As I watched the shimmering city lights down below I thought of my home in Wazir Bagh and wondered what my family was doing at that moment. Lying in that 'sardi ki dhoop' in our garden, could I ever have imagined my life would take so many turns?

When the plane landed, Mr Pottasch and I went to this very exclusive restaurant. He said a billionaire was probably seated at every table. I had to borrow his jacket because men weren't allowed in the restaurant without one.

While we were having dinner and a glass of fine wine, I told him a little secret about how I did not go to a good school or college, and learnt how to speak English only when I was sixteen. In those days, I talked with an American accent. It was a mix of Clark Gable in *Gone with the Wind* and Marlon Brando in *On the Waterfront*. When we got a little high, Alan asked:

How come you're so fair? You don't look very Indian.
Alan, Kashmiris are fair-skinned. And I'm 100 per cent Indian!
But you don't look like one. You think like me and you sound like me . . .
My accent sounds like yours because I learnt my English watching Hollywood movies!

We had a big laugh. Our friendship lasted a long time.

AJ: You did end up making some ads for ICICI Bank, didn't you?

VVC: After I made the Pepsi ad and it was successful, Mike Khanna, the biggest ad executive in India at the time, asked me if I wanted to make more ads. I said I'd come back to him if I was broke and needed money. He laughed and said he'd just have to wait.

In 1998, when *Kareeb* bombed, I called him and told him I was broke. Instead of sympathizing with me, he sounded delighted: 'That's the best news I've heard in a long, long time. Now you can make ads for us.'

That's how I made the ad for the launch of the ICICI Bank. When I met Mr K.V. Kamath, the chairman of ICICI, I asked for a crore.

Why are you asking for so much money?
Because you're a bank! And I need the money.
No one has ever said that before! How much will it actually cost?
Very little. But I need to save some money and make another feature film. My last film bombed, so I'm broke and that's why I'm making your ad.

My logic seemed to satisfy him and he agreed to pay me and he paid me well. With the money I had saved from the ad, I produced and directed *Mission Kashmir.*

AJ: What about *1942: A Love Story.* What made you want to make a period film?

VVC: The primary reason why I went back to 1942 was music. When I was making the film, music in Hindi cinema was going through a terrible crisis. All kinds of vulgar songs were being written and there was a real decline in the standard of music and lyrics, so I wanted to bring back beautiful music—the kind that I loved when I was growing up.

So I thought of making an intimate love story with a fine musical score—it was a story I wrote with Anu's mother, Kamna Chandra. Then we decided to give the film scale and used the freedom struggle as a backdrop. We went for a bigger challenge.

I think life without challenges is very boring. That was one of the reasons I made it into a period film and created a huge set at Film City. We built a whole town and created a lake—in fact it was one of the first times in Hindi film that anyone had made such a big set.

AJ: You talk most fondly of R.D. Burman. When you asked him to work on *1942*, I think you said you wanted his father's music and because S.D. Burman was no longer alive, you had come to him.

VVC: That's exactly what I said. RD was going through a bad patch. To the extent that HMV, the music company, told me: 'If you take a new guy, we'll pay well. If you take R.D. Burman, we may not buy the music.' Back then, there were very few music companies besides HMV that we could approach.

Do you know the story of 'Kuchh na kaho'?

AJ: I remember it went through many changes.

VVC: Yes. At first RD proposed a very different tune than the one we ended up with. I went to see him in his music room.

There was a huge photograph of S.D. Burman hanging on the wall and below the framed photograph of his father sat RD and his ten or twelve musicians. He played me a tune and asked me what I thought of it. I didn't want to be rude in the presence of all his musicians. So I said:

Let me think about it.
You never think about things. You always react immediately. What's your first reaction?

He could do better is something I should've said, but being the uncouth, undiplomatic guy that I am, I started by saying it's no good, then said it's rubbish and finally blurted out—it's bullshit!

By that time, all his musicians had left the room, one by one. RD had heard about HMV's comments, so he turned to me and asked if I wanted him to do *1942* at all. My immediate reaction was: 'Dada! You know I love you. Please don't blackmail me emotionally. I want you to compose the music but this is not the tune I'm looking for. Actually I'm looking for S.D. Burman. He's gone and I believe you are the best music director that this country has at this moment. But the music you're giving me is not it.'

When I think back to that day, I think the conversation we had was sad.

Vinod, you don't understand. The old music doesn't sell. This is what sells.
Leave the selling to me. I'm the producer. You don't need to worry about what sells and what doesn't. Just create the music.

Will you give me a week?

I'll give you a year, Dada. I'll wait a year but give me the music I want.

I'll never forget that day. Dada was wearing a blue silk lungi and kurta and when I was about to leave, I saw he had tears in his eyes. He became very emotional and so did I. We hugged each other very warmly as I said goodbye.

Just imagine how insecure he must have felt. I knew life had become difficult for him in his last years. Most of his friends and well-wishers had walked out on him, even the people he was very close to were gone. He was a very lonely man.

RD was the man who created some of the best music in Indian cinema and here he was doubting whether his music would sell. I mean he was R.D. Burman! A composer whom everyone adores today and has nothing but praise and admiration for. Though many years have passed, every Sunday I still see ads in the newspaper about shows with R.D. Burman's music.

I tell you, this film world can be unforgiving. It's heartless. I remember hearing Guru Dutt became depressed after the failure of *Kaagaz Ke Phool* and now the film is regarded as an outstanding piece of work.

AJ: What happened after that meeting with RD?

VVC: He asked me to come back a week later. The day I went back, his music room was empty. I sat waiting and wondered if he was going to say no to composing for *1942*.

But a few minutes later he walked in with a little cassette recorder in his hand and said: 'I've been listening to these S.D. Burman compositions but the tune is still not coming to me. I've made hundreds of tunes but I don't like any of them. Give me another week.'

Another week passed. I went back again and this time all his musicians were there, Babloo-da, Manohari-da and the others. Then RD started playing the tune of what we know now as 'Kuchh na kaho'.

When I'm working with a composer, I have this habit of listening to the tune with my eyes closed. If I like a tune, I raise my hand—it's a signal to the composer that all's good. RD was very familiar with the way I reacted to a song. So while he played the short musical prologue to 'Kuchh na kaho', I raised my hand with my eyes closed as usual. He stopped playing.

What did that sign mean?
It's very nice.
But the song hasn't started yet.
Dada, if these are your first notes, I know where the song is going.

From composing a rubbishy tune because he thought it was more commercial, he composed a magnificent melody that came from his heart. 'Kuchh na kaho' will never be forgotten. I'll always be very grateful to Dada for that melody.

AJ: Then you had Kumar Sanu sing it.

VVC: He was the number one singer then. On the day of the recording, we were waiting at Film Center in Tardeo for him to show up. RD and all the musicians sat patiently while I was getting agitated and wondered how much money was being wasted. In those days, the music was played live and the musicians were paid in four-hour shifts, so I knew our shift was soon coming to an end and there was still no sign of Kumar Sanu.

He finally showed up three hours late. As soon as he arrived, he went straight into the singers' cabin and started singing into the mic. He sang terribly. And I mean terribly! I looked at RD and said: 'Dada! He has no emotion in his voice. He's singing in tune but there's no life in his rendition.'

Dada was going to talk to Sanu in the recording cabin and I offered to go in with him. I'm sure he thought I would explode, so RD said: 'No, no, no. You stay here. Sanu is a big star. Don't come with me. We have no one else, he has to sing the song.'

I could hear RD from the recording room pleading with Sanu who kept saying: 'Dada, I was busy recording at Sunny's. I left the song halfway and came all the way from Juhu just for you. There are two more songs I have to record today. I have to leave soon. We have to finish the recording in half an hour.'

Dada was about to agree to rush through the recording when I lost my temper. I opened the door of the singers' cabin and could see Sanu sitting there, unshaven. He had clearly not slept for a few days. I asked him to leave the recording studio. Sanu was taken aback and asked Dada who I was, and before Dada could answer, I said:

'Go home. Rest. You look like a mess. We'll wait a week for you. Whenever you have a whole day, we'll record the song. If you don't have the time, never mind, we'll find someone else.'

R.D. Burman looked at Sanu and kept saying, 'No, no, Sanu . . .' I stopped RD and said: 'No. Dada, I have let the musicians go home. Their shift is over. Finished! I'll pay for this shift but I don't want the song to be recorded in a broken, tired voice.'

As I left the room, I turned around and told Sanu: 'By the way, I'm the producer and director of this film.'

To Sanu's credit, he came back to Film Center three days later. He had shaved and was looking well and rested. He presented me with a fountain pen and gave me a lovely smile: 'This is for you, Binod. Thank you for that day.' I thanked him and he recorded 'Kuchh na kaho'. This time he sang it brilliantly.

AJ: It's an incredible song. I believe Javed Akhtar struggled with the other song in *1942*, 'Chupke se'. I hear he went to Kaifi Azmi's place to write it.

VVC: Javed Sahib explained to me that the kind of songs *1942* deserved could not be written in a city because they needed a certain purity he could not find in the city. So, yes, he went to Azamgarh and in the quiet of Kaifi Sahib's home he wrote 'Chupke se'. He recited it to me over the phone a few days later. It was beautiful.

I miss all that. You know I miss that madness. Because most people were crazy. They pulled out all the stops, pushed themselves till they found better creative solutions. Money has become all important today and it has dampened the striving for perfection. I am grateful that at VVC Films we're still striving for excellence and that's all that matters.

AJ: What was it like working with Javed Sahib?

VVC: It was lovely. He strives for excellence in his own way.

The song 'Ek ladki ko dekha' had not been planned in the screenplay. But Javed Sahib kept saying there had to be a song at that point in the story.

After we recorded 'Ek ladki ko dekha', Javed Sahib admitted to me that the day he was coming to work with R.D. Burman and me on the tune, he had not written a single line. He left his house in Juhu and the first line came to him as he was passing Lido cinema, a few minutes' drive from his home. From Lido to RD's house in Khar, he had written the entire song. When he got to RD's place, he recited the lyrics while RD composed the tune on his harmonium. The song was done in minutes.

When you're creating something, honestly you have no idea what it can become and how far it will go. That was a magical day.

AJ: I'm sure RD knew the song was exceptional.

VVC: No, I don't think so. After we recorded it, RD called me the following day.

Yeh main wapas record karna chahta hoon. Bahut thin hai, yaar. [I want to record it again. It's very thin.]
Thin hai? [Thin?]
Tang tang tang . . . then it goes 'Ek ladki ko dekha to aisa laga'. It's empty. It's thin. I want to add some strings. Something else . . .

I knew if he tried recording the song again, he'd do something terrible because he was so insecure. So I lied: 'Dada! You're only hearing the main track. I'm going to add sound effects. A car moving, a train passing, wind blowing. All that emptiness will be filled by sound effects.'

I somehow convinced him and the song survived.

AJ: During the making of *1942*, you had a problem with the film association? I forget what it was called then.

VVC: You mean the Film Makers Combine, FMC? It was made up of some very powerful producers, distributors and exhibitors and was the strongest body that had ever controlled the film industry.

There was some dispute going on between the workers and producers. So the producers announced that no payment should be made to the workers unless they accepted a lower wage or something like that—I honestly don't remember exactly what it was about, but when I paid my workers for Diwali for the *1942* shoot, they banned me from filming.

The FMC controlled the equipment hire and everything else. I ended up living in a make-up room at Film City for thirty-two days. I didn't leave the place. Mr Govind Swaroop, who was secretary in the Maharashtra government and who was in charge of Film City, made sure the cops and the security guys there did not allow any outsiders to come to our set. He protected me, otherwise I would not have been able to shoot.

The final shoot days were a complete disaster—my actors were heckled and I was told I could not release the film because they were going to ban it. I asked them to let me make the film, even if it would never be released. Two or three of FMC's leading members—I won't name them; they have all passed away—asked me what was the use of making a film I could not release. This was more or less our exchange:

> Please let me finish the film. I'll give it to you in writing that I won't release my film.
> *So why make it if you can't release it?*
> I'll wait till you guys die. Then I'll release it.

I'm not surprised they were furious with me!

One of the reasons I couldn't film the climax of the film as I had planned was because I didn't have what I needed. The FMC created many problems for us. So five or six directors I knew came to help me out. The end sequence was shot with multiple cameras because we had a crowd of about two or three thousand people just for the day. I remember Shekhar Kapur directed the shots of Danny Denzongpa on a horse.

AJ: I believe you also faced another challenge—in changing Anil Kapoor's look in *1942*.

VVC: Oh, yes! Anil had long hair and I wanted him to cut it. It was difficult for him because he was acting in many other films at the same time and cutting his hair would've created continuity problems. He was a big star and there was no way he was going to cut his hair short. His brother Boney Kapoor was extremely upset at the very thought, maybe because he had no idea how Anil would look with short hair.

We had a shooting schedule in Dalhousie so I left for the location and a few days later Anil joined me. He called me to his hotel room and opened the door with his back to me. He was wearing a cap, and when he turned around, I could see he had cut his hair! He looked amazing. I don't think he grew his hair long after that. He looked much younger with short hair.

AJ: It's been over twenty-six years since *1942: A Love Story* was released and the songs from the film are still very popular. They haven't dated at all.

I believe the film did very well overseas, especially in London.

VVC: Oh, yes! We were staying at the Cumberland Hotel in Marble Arch and from our hotel window, we could see a long winding queue that started in a side street and went all the way to the Odeon ticket counter. My overseas distributor, Kishore Lulla, was very excited and told me he had never seen such big crowds for an Indian film before.

1942 was the first film made in India that had Dolby sound. There were only mono films till then. But I insisted on Dolby, so we had to go to London for the final audio mix. We hired a truck from Heathrow airport to carry about 300 cans of picture and sound with us. Before I left Bombay, Manmohan Shetty was shocked and said: 'Are you mad? Why are you recording in Dolby? There are no cinemas in India with Dolby sound. How are you going to project your film?'

He was right. There were no cinemas with Dolby sound in the 1990s apart from Sterling in Fort, where we held our trial shows. So I personally paid for temporary Dolby wiring at the Metro because the theatre owners refused to pay for it. They thought it was a waste of money. I believe *1942* opened doors for Dolby in India.

AJ: You were incredibly ambitious.

VVC: More ambitious than I am now! I have mellowed with age. [*both smile*]

AJ: Going back to R.D. Burman—did he get to see *1942*?

VVC: He passed away before the movie and the music were released. That was heartbreaking.

He saw the songs, including 'Ek ladki ko dekha', while I was editing, but he did not live to see the tremendous impact his music would have. It was a Van Gogh moment for me. RD had created great music, but died before he could know how many millions appreciated his work all over again. That is one of my great regrets. I wish Dada had lived longer.

AJ: Isn't there a story about him visiting the set and you had a surprise party for him?

VVC: It was actually a New Year's Eve party. I threw a big bash on the sets of *1942*. The alcohol ran out in half an hour! Jackie Shroff paid for the evening. He is a generous guy. There were thousands of gate-crashers because everyone on every set at Film City knew we were having a party.

We were waiting for RD to come before we lit the fireworks because we wanted the evening to be a celebration of his music. At around 11 p.m. Dada arrived. He parked his car and started walking over to the set as we played 'Ek ladki ko dekha' over the loudspeakers and the fireworks lit up the sky. He was wearing a white shirt, his usual red muffler around his neck and a little cap on his head. He looked very handsome walking slowly down the slope to the set.

So, he did hear his music with thousands of partygoers clapping for him. On 4 January 1994, four days later, he passed away.

I'm grateful to have spent time with so many wonderful people. They have enriched my life. I have very few friends but they all matter to me. I feel a lot of our life is lived among acquaintances. I think I've been blessed. Anu once asked me what I wanted to do for my birthday, I said: 'Will Abhijat come over? We'll sit and chat.'

AJ: I remember that lovely evening. We had a great time.

I have worked with you on films you've directed and on films you've produced. How was the transition from director to producer for you? I sense you're a reluctant producer.

VVC: Very reluctant. I hate producing. I became a producer because of Raju Hirani. When Renu Saluja was editing *Mission Kashmir*, she fell critically ill and passed away. She was suffering from cancer. It was devastating.

So I asked Raju to edit the film. While he was editing, he narrated the idea of *Munna Bhai M.B.B.S.* to me. I got involved with the script and helped him to write it. Before I knew it, I offered to produce it. I had no plans of becoming a producer.

Even today, producing is not something that excites me very much. I only produce films I believe need me as a producer. Films that would not have been made otherwise. This was the case with all the films we have produced — *Munna Bhai M.B.B.S.*, *Parineeta*, *Ferrari ki Sawaari* and *Wazir*. They did not look like commercial ventures but they all did pretty well at the box office.

AJ: I have noticed you're never on the sets of a film you're producing. Has that always been the case?

VVC: It was during the first film I produced, *Munna Bhai M.B.B.S.*, that I decided not to go on the sets of another director. When I went to Raju Hirani's set, instead of looking at Raju to okay a take, Sanjay Dutt kept turning to me and asking: 'Kaisa hai, sir-ji?' [How was it, sir?]

When I left the *Munna Bhai* set that day I told Raju that I wasn't coming back. As a director, I would hate for such a thing to happen to me. The director is the god of the film and not the damn producer.

AJ: You've produced five Raju Hirani films, haven't you?

VVC: I have no idea.

AJ: Let's see—there was *Munna Bhai M.B.B.S.*, *Lage Raho Munna Bhai*, *3 Idiots*, *PK* and *Sanju*.

VVC: Raju will always be the dearest to me because he was my first cinema kid in a way. He's an exceptional human being. His wife once joked with me and said: 'All the other guys get cards on Valentine's Day and this guy gets cards on Gandhi Jayanti!'

I enjoyed writing with him and helping him whenever I could, particularly on *Munna Bhai M.B.B.S.* and *Lage Raho Munna Bhai*.

I co-wrote *Parineeta* with Pradeep Sarkar, who directed the film. It was fun working with him. When he showed me his script, I knew it was based on Sarat Chandra Chatterjee's story. I asked him:

Why are you using the story as an inspiration, why not just remake *Parineeta*?
Sir, Parineeta *flopped twice. Bimal Roy's version and then Ajoy Kar's 1969 version, both films flopped.*

I reassured Pradeep Sarkar that I was fine about producing it, if he had the courage to direct it.

Abhijat, just imagine, we were producing a movie that had flopped twice! That was really dumb. [*both laugh*]

AJ: I think the strength of Pradeep Sarkar's visuals convinced you to produce *Parineeta.*

VVC: Yes. Pradeep Sarkar is from Bengal and knew that milieu well. He also has a very good musical sense. His budget sense, however, like most other directors, was not so good.

I'll give you an example of how you can work within budget and not undermine the integrity of the film.

Bejoy called me during the *Wazir* shoot and said: 'I have a silly question. We're shooting a scene with Farhan Akhtar at a school. We need at least sixty kids in the background and we have to get them uniforms. The uniforms will cost a lakh and a half.'

I waited a minute before I said: 'That's a waste of money! Why would I spend a lakh and a half on uniforms for kids who are visible in the background? Why have Farhan meet the heroine in a school at all? Get a dog. Raju Hirani has a dog. It's a free dog! Have the heroine take her dog for a walk, and the hero, who also has a dog, meets her on his walk.' There was a long silence and then Bejoy finally said: 'I knew you'd come up with something.'

The point is, there's always another way to film a scene. Bejoy found a school where we didn't have to pay for uniforms. So it was a happy ending all round. At the risk of repeating myself, I'll say again, if you spend more than you have budgeted, you'll have to recover a lot more and be obliged to compromise and forced to make films you aren't proud of.

AJ: When you talk about staying within budget, I think you learnt that lesson early in your career.

VVC: Oh, yes! It dates back to when we made *Khamosh*. Kundan Shah was one of the co-writers and he got really mad at me about Naseer's entry in the film.

For Naseer's entry, I planned a shot with him sitting in a bus. Kundan Shah and Ranjit Kapoor, who was the dialogue writer on *Khamosh*, came up with the idea that the bus should meet with an accident. The bus overturns dramatically and lands on its side. The door flies open and out comes Naseer, the gallant hero, who helps the injured passengers. It was a great introduction but I refused to listen to them. 'Nahin yaar, ye bilkul theek hai, bus mein aise baitha hai.' [No, my friends, Naseer's entry is fine. Let's just see him sitting in the bus.]

Kundan piped up: 'It's damn boring, yaar, he's just sitting in a bus?'

I tried another tactic: 'My camera will be circling around him and we'll see great views of Kashmir.' Kundan and Ranjit didn't give up and kept insisting in turn:

But why aren't you listening to us? We have a much better idea! Imagine a bus driving along and it has a violent accident. Our hero is the first man to get out of the bus and help the injured. That's a proper hero's entry! *You know how much it'll cost to overturn a bus?*

That's not the way to write. You're corrupt! Your mind is corrupt. You're only thinking of the cost.
I have to. Because that's how we'll make this film. If I spend extra money turning the bus over, I won't have any money to shoot the rest of the movie!

The most important lesson I learnt was, if you want to make honest cinema you must be mindful of your budget—I think it's probably because I grew up in a lower-middle-class family that I think like that. If you go over budget, you might end up making films that are basically shitty.

AJ: Was *Jaane Bhi Do Yaaro* a difficult film to produce?

VVC: The film was made in the editing room because Kundan kept shooting and shooting.

I remember we were filming in the NFDC guest house at Breach Candy. I had booked a bus to go to Alibaug at six the following morning. I held off paying the bus owner because I knew Kundan would keep shooting and was not going to leave on time. But Kundan kept reassuring me he'd be on that bus at 6 a.m. I asked Renu if he was being realistic and she said:

6 a.m. departure? Impossible.
Will he be ready at 10?
A hundred per cent.

I paid the bus guy his money. But what finally happened? Kundan and his crew shot the whole night and stopped at two the next afternoon. There's a photograph somewhere of Binod Pradhan, leaning on the camera viewfinder, fast asleep. The poor guy had fallen asleep between takes! He was that exhausted. *Jaane Bhi Do Yaaro* was a crazy experience.

AJ: Do you think film-makers are aware of production costs when they're writing their screenplays?

VVC: Not many are. That's why I feel my interaction with young directors is important. Hopefully, they'll learn this golden lesson—restrict your budget to hold on to your freedom!

AJ: When we first met during the production of *Kareeb*, and before I started co-writing the film with you, I remember you asked me to make sure every scene had a purpose because two lakhs were allotted to each shoot day and you said if I took out four unnecessary scenes, we'd save eight lakhs.

I also recall when Mr Bachchan's office asked for a special hotel room for the Rajasthan shoot of *Eklavya*, you politely said it wasn't doable. I think the room would have cost 65,000 rupees more than you had in the budget for his accommodation. The SMS you sent him is worth mentioning here: 'I don't like surprises,' it read. [*both laugh*] Mr Bachchan graciously paid for the room himself.

VVC: I wanted to repay his many gestures of generosity to me, including the fact that he did not walk out on me when

I shouted at him during the shoot of *Eklavya*, and for taking me on a private plane ride. That's why I gifted him a Rolls-Royce Phantom after the release of *Eklavya*.

My mother and I went together to Mr Bachchan's house to give him the keys of the Rolls and as we were returning home in my rickety blue Maruti van, she said: 'You bloody fool! You gave him such a big car, why don't you buy yourself a new car, Vidhu? You're driving around in this old *khatara*.' After a thoughtful pause, she added: 'That car must have cost at least eleven lakhs.'

I nodded yes—eleven lakhs. I didn't have the heart to tell her it cost over four crores! She tapped my shoulder affectionately and said: 'You go and buy Lambu [that's what she called Amitabh] an eleven-lakh car and drive a piece of old junk yourself! You crazy boy! Buy yourself a new car.'

AJ: What was the budget of *Munna Bhai M.B.B.S.*?

VVC: I don't remember the exact budget. But I handed Raju a cheque book and said: 'Go, make your movie.' The credit goes to Raju because he spent the budget wisely.

AJ: Raju told me something amusing about the wedding scene in *Munna Bhai M.B.B.S.*

VVC: That story has to go in this book!

There was a wedding scene in the film and we did not want to spend a lot of money on a set because all the script required was a series of stills showing the married couple, Sanjay and Gracy, and nothing else.

So, our team went to a real wedding. They congratulated the newly-weds and then they sat waiting for the couple to be greeted by their family and guests. The bride and bridegroom usually sit on throne-like chairs and when they left, Sanjay and Gracy Singh took their seats. A photographer quickly shot all the stills we needed for the film. [*both laugh*]

AJ: I think Raju figured he didn't need to get expensive wedding clothes made either, so I believe they rented them. Gracy Singh apparently complained to Sanjay Dutt about this and Sanju was angry and said: 'If that's how it is, I'll buy the wedding clothes.'

VVC: And I hear Raju told him: 'Go ahead. We don't have the budget for wedding clothes.'

AJ: How did Raju and you go about writing *Munna Bhai M.B.B.S.*?

VVC: We sat in my study and basically talked about the scenes—did they work or didn't they? Our sessions were recorded and Raju later referred to the audio files as he wrote the screenplay and dialogues with his team. That's how I normally work, even today.

Remind me, Abhijat, at what stage did you join Raju on the writing of *Lage Raho*?

AJ: Raju had developed the idea of *Lage Raho* entirely on his own. Six months after he started writing, I joined him.

I suggested that Gandhi-ji should not be a ghost, but a hallucination in Munna's head—a chemical locha. I also suggested we use the radio to spread 'Gandhigiri'. But it was completely Raju's idea that the movie should be about Munna and Mahatma Gandhi-ji.

What I find admirable is your refusal to make 'Munna Bhai 3' until you are convinced that you have a good script. You could make millions, even with a mediocre script, considering it's such a popular franchise—but you won't.

VVC: You're right. We could make a lot of money with a third Munna Bhai. People say we're mad. But we must continue to make cinema we believe in. I'm sure the commercial world thinks we're really crazy that we are not making another Munna Bhai. Maybe we're crazy but we're happy and fulfilled!

AJ: I suppose it's a satisfying feeling to think we made some of the biggest hits, yet our decisions were not based on commercial priorities.

VVC: That's something I'm very proud of.

AJ: On a completely different tack, I wanted to ask you if you're a religious person?

VVC: Not in the traditional sense. I strongly believe there is some power we cannot fathom. For example, in this room, there are ultraviolet and infrared rays, but we cannot see them. Our vision is limited. I believe there's something beyond us that we cannot see.

I'm as much a Christian, a Muslim, a Sikh as a Hindu in my thinking—whatever the contradiction. Every time I go to Europe, I pray in the splendid churches there. I can feel the vibe of years of prayer within those walls. Religion to me is respecting the unknown.

AJ: I know there are many facets to your personality that people don't know about. Is there something we've not discussed?

VVC: I've given very few interviews in my life. So people don't really know much about me. There is something I haven't talked about to many people, maybe not even to you.

When I was at the FTII, I did not want to get ragged. I bought a swordstick dagger in Kashmir. It's called a 'gupti'. The knife is usually concealed in a wooden casing, which has the outer appearance of a short stick. All through my FTII days, I kept that knife in my pocket. The other students discovered that I carried it with me at all times and because of that no one ragged me. They thought I was crazy. When a new batch of students joined, I made sure they were not ragged either—it was the fear of that knife that put the bullies off. I never used it.

When I left Pune, which was a smaller city in those days, and came to Bombay to live, I used to suffer from anxiety. I had spent all my life in Kashmir and I was not used to crowds. Seeing so many poor people living on the streets and in slums made me very uncomfortable. Poverty disturbed me. I thought I had to do something in my own little way.

One day I saw this young boy begging on Linking Road at Khar and asked him to come and live with Renu and me. Far from owning our own home, we ourselves were paying guests. I knew I couldn't rid the world of poverty, but at least I could help this one boy. So he came and stayed with us. I bought him some clothes and found a municipal school for him. But all the while, he was sure we wanted him to work for us in exchange. He was quite confused and kept asking:

Do I have to cook? Do I have to wash dishes?
You don't have to do anything, you'll just study.

I had only one possession of any value and that was a tape recorder and a few tapes of Begum Akhtar that I'd listen to every evening. A few days after he had moved in with us, I came home to find the little bugger had stolen the tape recorder and run away. I was so enraged that I took my long knife and went in search of him. I went everywhere looking for him but could not find him.

That same day Renu was spending time with her friend, Uttama Rashk, the daughter of the film writer Arjun Dev Rashk, so I joined her later that night. They were living somewhere in Khar. When they saw me, both Renu and Uttama started laughing and said: 'Just look at your face.'

I thought I had some dirt stuck on my cheek or something. I looked in the mirror and found nothing.

I had very long hair and I was very thin then. Renu started laughing again and said: 'You look like a man who has come out of a mental asylum.' Uttama joined in: 'You'll meet many people in Bombay who will con you. If you stay in this city, you'll no longer be the Kashmiri Vinod you are, you'll become someone else.'

This incident happened about forty-five years ago. And since then I have been conned and cheated many times. But I do not allow negative experiences to change me. I choose not to think that everyone is out to cheat. When we encounter dishonest people, we often become dishonest in order to protect ourselves. We become less humane, less empathetic. Thanks to Renu and Uttama, I did not let the incident with the street kid change who I was.

AJ: Wasn't it a criminal offence to go around with a knife?

VVC: Yes, of course! And I could have been arrested and thrown in jail. But I was young and in many ways I was crazy.

AJ: I've known you for so many years, but I didn't know about this incident. Did it teach you something?

VVC: The lesson I learnt that day reminded me of my childhood. Come to think of it, my father may not have spoken to me as an equal in the way that my children and I talk to each other—but he instilled in me a deep sense of morality, particularly through the stories he told me. Those stories became the principles by which I have lived.

AJ: Which story are you thinking of?

VVC: My father once told me about a sadhu who had a beautiful white horse. A dacoit wanted that horse badly. He tried very hard to buy it from the sadhu, but the sadhu refused to sell it to him.

One day when the sadhu was riding somewhere, he saw an old man on the road. He was clearly suffering from leprosy and could hardly walk. He looked at the sadhu with exhausted eyes, and out of compassion, the sadhu got off the majestic white horse and asked the old man to mount it. The minute the old man took hold of the reins, the sadhu realized he was not an old frail man but the dacoit. The dacoit laughed and before galloping off, he said: 'I asked you to sell the horse to me, but you refused. Now I'm taking it.'

A few days later, the sadhu made his way to the dacoit's den. When the dacoit saw him, he was certain the holy man had come to reclaim his horse. The dacoit laughed and asked sarcastically:

Have you come to reclaim your horse?
No.
Then why are you here?
Please don't tell anyone about what happened.
So, have you come to ask me not to tell people just how foolish you are, O great saint?
That is not the reason I'm here. If you tell people what happened, no one will ever trust anyone suffering from leprosy again. So let it remain a secret between us.

The sadhu then walked all the way home. The next morning he heard his majestic white horse neighing outside his window. The sadhu stepped out and saw his horse had returned. The sadhu's eyes filled with tears. The tears fell into the wet soil and mixed with the tears of the dacoit.

AJ: What a beautiful story. [*long pause*] It's philosophical and poetic. You tell stories so well!

I know that poetry interests you too.

VVC: You've reminded me of an evening I spent with Pran Sahib during the shooting of *1942* in Dalhousie. I was reciting Ghalib and he was taken aback and asked:

> You know Urdu?
> *Sir, I grew up in a small place in Kashmir.*
> I never thought you knew Ghalib. You behave like an angrez!

He hugged me. Frankly, I didn't know that Pran Sahib was into Urdu poetry either. We had such a blast that evening.

AJ: I can see from the time you made your diploma film, you've been pushing the envelope. In 2014, you went out of your comfort zone and took the brave decision of directing *Broken Horses* in America, an English-language film with American actors. Why?

VVC: Why? You were with me from the start, yaar! Remember, we were travelling by train to Boston for a screening of *Eklavya*? We had just seen Martin Scorsese's film *The Departed* and I told you it was based on the Hong Kong film *Infernal Affairs*, which I thought was a better film than Scorsese's.

At that time, we were discussing the idea of doing the Mahabharata in English for a Western audience. I felt they should know about our culture. I went to the bar on the train to buy us a beer and when I came back, you said: 'Why don't we remake *Parinda*?' I thought it was a damn good idea and that's how it started.

As you know, *Parinda* was set in Bombay and *Broken Horses*—actually that wasn't the title then—was to be set in New York. So we rented an apartment in New York, I think it was in Sutton Place, and we wrote the first draft there.

Michael Lynton, the head of Sony Studio, introduced me to Nicholas Pileggi, on whose non-fiction book *Wiseguy*, Scorsese's *Goodfellas* was based. So we sent the script to Pileggi and asked him for an honest opinion. Nick said he'd get back to us the following Thursday, i.e., two days later.

Two nights before our meeting, we went for a stroll to the Rockefeller Center. I was talking to you about a murder scene I had imagined taking place there—people are skating on white ice and suddenly drops of blood appear on the ice—a guy bumps into another guy and his head rolls off. His throat has been slit. Everybody stares in horror at this dismembered body. Then we see a man slowly walking away.

We talked excitedly about this murder scene when I stopped a passer-by and asked:

Is this Sixth Avenue? Because we've just passed Fifth Avenue.

No, this is Park Lane.

Then I mistook another avenue for Broadway. By the time we got back to the flat, I remember telling you: 'You know what? We can't do this film in New York. I don't know this city. I'd have to live here for many years before we could make a film here. Martin Scorsese makes his films here because this is his city. People will laugh at us. They'll say, "Oh, Bollywood comes to Hollywood and makes this shit."'

That happened on a Tuesday night. Early on Wednesday morning around 6 a.m.—that's when I get most of my ideas—I decided not to set the story in New York, but instead we should use elements of nature as backdrop— earth, water, wind, etc. Use universal elements and forget about New York, a city I didn't even know.

I could never know American culture like an American film-maker who was born and brought up there. How could I? In the same way, he could not know Indian culture. He would not know the pulse of Bombay or Kashmir. But we've all experienced fire, water, earth and wind. That was my rationale.

So you and I started writing a new film. We worked flat out for forty-eight hours. On Thursday, at around 5 p.m., Nick Pileggi arrived with a bunch of papers in his hand. He sat on the sofa and said:

I've read your draft and I have some comments about how you see New York.

Nick, before you give me your notes, we've done some work I'd like to share with you.

I narrated our new script to him. He didn't react to any scene—he did not say if he liked it or not. We were silent—actually, we were completely exhausted, not having slept for two nights. Pileggi heard us out and finally said: 'The approach you're taking reminds me of another film-maker I met. He did not know English as well as you do. I met him in Italy and in poor English he explained his film to me in the way you just did and I could see the whole movie. You must have heard of him. Sergio Leone?'

Abhijat, you had started walking towards the kitchen at that point, but when you heard the name 'Sergio Leone', you cried out in Hindi to me: 'Thok diya!' [We've cracked it!] That was the beginning of *Broken Horses*.

AJ: I remember we travelled with the well-known cinematographer Pawel Edelman for thousands of miles across America looking for locations. In the end, Pawel did not photograph *Broken Horses,* Tom Stern did. Remind me of how you first thought of filming in New Mexico.

VVC: We were in Albuquerque and the next morning we had a flight back to LA. I saw this place called Lordsburg, New Mexico, on the Net, and I thought: 'I gotta go there.'

My location manager came to my room at seven o'clock so we would leave on time for the airport. When he entered our hotel room, my assistant told him there was a change in the programme. 'Vinod wants to go to Lordsburg.' He looked at me and said anxiously:

> No, no, no . . . we can't go to Lordsburg—it's four or five hundred miles from here. We'll never get back in time for the flight.
> *I have to go there.*
> What about your 9 a.m. flight?
> *I don't give a damn, I must go to Lordsburg.*

He headed towards the door. I thought he was going to walk out on us. I asked him where he was going. He said: 'I'm getting some cold drinks for you guys. It's a long drive.'

We drove twelve to sixteen hours—all over Arizona, New Mexico, you name it, we went everywhere. When you have a passion for something that comes from within you, nothing seems like a trial. And I was crazy enough to think we could shoot the whole film in Lordsburg. Pawel Edelman, who had worked with the Polish director Andrzej Wajda, and whom I deeply respected, reminded me that Lordsburg was in the middle of nowhere and filming there would be a production nightmare. Pawel was clear: 'If you decide to shoot on this location, I don't think I can do it.'

I wondered what was wrong with him—it was just a location. But then I realized it was a mad choice.

AJ: Was working in America a big change for you?

VVC: It was a big change and not a subtle one, it was brutal. I had to learn a new cinematic language.

As you know, Indian cinema comes from the tradition of the Urdu–Parsi theatre, which is basically loud and melodramatic. The older Indian films were mostly over-the-top melodrama. One line of dialogue is repeated five times and the emotion is always heightened. It's a completely different style.

So coming from that tradition, the struggle for me was how do I tone myself down? How do I direct American actors differently? Changing my method of working was difficult. It's like asking a football player to play cricket.

AJ: I know it was a tightrope for you because you did not want to lose the unique something you were bringing to the table.

VVC: I didn't want to lose my roots or the cinematic tradition I came from and that played a part in my choice of story, which was about two brothers. This is a storyline very popular in Hindi films. In *Broken Horses*, one brother is involved with the mafia, drugs and trafficking and the other is a violin player. It was an intentional reworking of *Parinda.*

If I ignored my roots, I knew I'd end up losing the uniqueness of the film. It would just become a dumb imitation of Hollywood. That said, directing *Broken Horses* was walking into unknown territory in every way. Working on the music was also new. I worked with John Debney, who wrote the music for *The Passion of Christ* and later for *The Jungle Book*. We recorded our soundtrack in Macedonia in Europe. It was the first time I'd worked with a choir and orchestra. It was not the sitar and tabla and the handful of musicians that I was used to. It was a completely different experience.

What I really enjoyed most was directing all the actors, including Vincent D'Onofrio, Chris Marquette and the late Anton Yelchin. They had a different approach to acting because they are trained in realistic cinema unlike most Indian actors. I was being challenged by these highly accomplished people every minute of the day and had to answer the questions they asked. It wasn't easy!

One day we were shooting a critical scene and Vincent was all over the place. Chris was really getting annoyed, so I asked him:

> Do you want me to tell Vincent to leave the room? Is he bothering you?
> *I want him to bother me. The character he's playing is someone I hate in the story, so if he keeps irritating me, it'll help my performance.*

Vincent D'Onofrio is a very different kind of actor. He kept fooling around on set but internally he was always thinking about his character. I gave him a long lecture about him being used to acting on TV and the need to think of big-screen acting—that comment annoyed him, especially if I happened to tell him between takes: 'That's TV, Vincent, we're making cinema here!'

AJ: I remember a scene you were filming—a fire is raging, it's really hot and the actors had to stand in that heat. And you went to Vincent and told him to remember that this was a movie. Vincent couldn't believe you said that, so he turned to Chris and mumbled: 'Did you hear what that son of a bitch just said?' Before Chris could react, you shouted, 'Action!'

VVC: [*laughs*] That was Vincent's best take because he was mad at me. I did that intentionally.

AJ: I saw an interview with Vincent D'Onofrio on YouTube. I think it may surprise you to know that he said he enjoyed working on *Broken Horses* because he felt 'directed' and hadn't felt that in a long time!

Werner Herzog also saw *Broken Horses* and liked it very much. That must have made you happy.

VVC: I couldn't believe his reaction to the film—he isn't someone who talks a lot but he hugged me and said we were brothers.

AJ: When Herzog came to see the film, he decided to stay for dinner. We all knew he hated eating in restaurants, so we ordered takeaway. Chris and Anton were there too, and your sister Shelly as well. I was supposed to go back to India that evening and you had my ticket cancelled. It must have cost about a lakh to cancel it, but you insisted I stayed—you said I could not miss an evening like that. It was indeed very special.

VVC: You know, he and I share a birthday, 5 September? Though Herzog is ten years my senior. I had seen all his films at film school. He belongs to the pantheon of cinema.

AJ: Besides Herzog, you also met another great film-maker, Alfonso Cuarón, who made wonderful films including *Y Tu Mama Tambien, Gravity*, among others.

VVC: We were on the jury of the Prague International Festival and we had a habit of taking a nap in the afternoon. We were the only two people on the jury who took a siesta out on the lawn. One day, just as it was time to get up, it started drizzling. I looked around and saw Alfonso still lying on the grass. I said:

> My friend, it's drizzling.
> *Yeah, I'm waiting for you to run. I don't want to run first.*

We had a good laugh, got up and ran back to the viewing theatre.

When Alfonso came to India I took him to Sanjay Leela Bhansali's *Devdas* set. He was quite fascinated by the way we made films. He was in the process of finding finance for *Y Tu Mama Tambien.* I had some money and suggested to him: 'Why don't you make the film in Goa? Nobody will know it's not Mexico. The beach will look the same. You bring your actors here and I'll get you the equipment you need and finance your film.' Alfonso got the funding he needed to make his film in Mexico. But he was kind enough to remember my offer.

When his Harry Potter film was premiering in New York in 2004, Anu asked me to request Alfonso for tickets. I was very reluctant to call him on the day of the premiere, but I did and asked for one ticket. He immediately said:

'No, bring the whole family.' So a group of us went to the premiere. He had given us the best seats in the house. I was sitting next to the actors, and after the screening, he invited us to join him for dinner at the top table. Alfonso values friendships and that means a lot to me. He's a good man.

AJ: I remember you telling me about meeting some great directors at the International Film Festival in Delhi.

VVC: Yes, in 1977, Michelangelo Antonioni, Elia Kazan, Akira Kurosawa and Satyajit Ray came to Delhi to attend the festival. For us film students it was the biggest high of the decade! I was overwhelmed. I sat at Kurosawa's feet and asked him how he went about writing a script. He spoke mostly in Japanese and had an interpreter by his side. He looked at me and said in English: 'Fade in (pause). Write, write, write!' He repeated the word 'write' a few more times, took a long pause and said: 'Fade out!' Kurosawa then said a few more words in Japanese to the interpreter. She translated his words for me: 'That, he says, is the only way to write a script.' It felt like a guru teaching a disciple how to write.

The encounter with Elia Kazan was also very instructive. I was very slim in those days, while he was a big strong man with the physique of a wrestler. He asked me what I wanted to do in life. I told him I wanted to be a film director like him. He hit my shoulder so hard that I lost my balance. He said: 'Look at you! You want to direct a movie? First you got to be tough like me!' He taught me that I had to look after my body and be physically fit if I wanted to direct films. Thanks to Elia Kazan I exercise six days a week to this day.

Antonioni was a completely different story. He was very high-strung and hardly spoke to the students. But I insisted:

> It's not fair, sir. Your film *L'Avventura* disturbed me a lot.
> I really need an answer from you.
> *Did I disturb you? Or did my movie disturb you?*
> Your movie, of course.
> *Then you have to look for an answer in my movie. Don't ask me.*

And he walked away.

AJ: What about Satyajit Ray?

VVC: He told us students something I won't forget: 'In my film or Ritwik Ghatak's film, if a crow crosses the sky by some fluke, there are students who will sit back and try to analyse the shot. "Oh! Why did a crow fly by at that moment?" But there's a hell of a lot that happens in a film because it just happens.'

Attending that 1977 film festival was a crazy learning experience, sitting at the feet of those great masters of cinema.

AJ: Then many years later you met James Cameron.

VVC: The circumstances were very different. I met him in New Delhi during a conclave. He read the script of *Broken Horses*. Liked it. And called me to talk about it.

When the film was nearly done, he screened the film in his private theatre. He was sitting in the front row and I was sitting right at the back. It was a large theatre and I was making notes since I was in the final stages of the edit. As the movie finished, and even before the lights went up, he started clapping. He clapped all the way from the first row to the back and said something to me on the lines of: 'You come from another culture, you've come out of your comfort zone and you've made something that's an artistic triumph.'

He made me realize how important it is to encourage other film-makers. Now when I meet young directors in India who are doing good work, I go out of my way to encourage them. Cameron was so gracious and gave us a quote to use to publicize the film.

AJ: Despite the fact that *Broken Horses* did not do well commercially, it sounds like it was a great experience for you and your cast.

VVC: That it was. When the shooting schedule was over and I was leaving for India, the crew gave me a book with pictures and handwritten messages. They told me what a wonderful experience making *Broken Horses* had been. Truly, it was a wonderful experience—though I wish I had made a better film.

AJ: Let's talk about your wife, Anupama. How did you both meet?

VVC: Sometime in the late 1980s, I got a telephone call from this young-sounding journalist who introduced herself as Anupama Chandra. She said she wanted to interview me for an article she was doing on the directors of the future. I said: 'Do you know anything about my past? Do you know who I am?'

She went quiet while I ranted on: 'Next time you call a film director, find out what they've made before. Don't make blind phone calls. I'm a National Award winner and my film was nominated for an Oscar. So if you ever write an article on the directors of the past, call me.' I was very rude to her. She must have thought, who the hell is this arrogant guy?

Anupama then went away to Northwestern University in Chicago to study journalism. *Parinda* was released in many cities around the world and when she noticed it was playing in Chicago, she remembered my cocky telephone conversation and went to see the film. She loved it and asked her mother, the writer Kamna Chandra, to meet me and see if she could work with me.

I was working on *1942: A Love Story* when Kamna-ji and I met. I had no idea she was the mother of the girl who had called me for an interview. We decided to work together on the screenplay of *1942*. And I finally met Anu when she returned to India.

Many months after our first meeting, Anu told me she was the one who had called me for an interview and reminded me how rude I was to her. See how destiny works! She called me for an interview, I was arrogant and rude, she saw *Parinda* in America, she told her mother to come and work with me, and one thing led to another . . .

When it came to watching the trial show of *1942: A Love Story*, I booked Sterling cinema and there Anu and I sat alone in the stalls. Kamna-ji, Shabnam Sukhdev's mother and my mother were sitting in the balcony. I think they suspected something was going on between us, and they were right. We were in love and ended up marrying in Madh Island on 1 June 1996. [*smiles*]

As far as our families go, the Chopras and the Chandras get on very well but ultimately the secret of our marriage is that Anu is a very caring person. Marrying her has been the best thing that's ever happened to me. I can't believe I've been faithful to one woman for almost twenty-five years. I was not a faithful kind of guy.

AJ: You both also share a great love for cinema. I'm wondering if you show her your film while you're editing.

VVC: No, she sees the film when it's done. The only time I ask for her advice is when it comes to English. My English is very bad. If I need a caption for the film, I'll get her to check it. Most people don't understand that her being a film critic means we keep our work lives separate. I don't rely on her to help me make my films, and she doesn't rely on me to write her film reviews. Period.

AJ: I have a feeling your children will be surprised to read about all the things you've lived through when they read this book.

VVC: I wonder how they'll react. Quite often, we can't tell what our children will take away from our behaviour.

The other day, Zuni reminded me of an incident that made an impression on her. Something I had totally forgotten. We had gone to Kashmir for a holiday and were having a picnic near Manasbal Lake. I wanted to use the public toilet, so she and I headed there. There was a guy outside the toilet who said I could not go in without paying two rupees. I didn't know why he wanted money and I told him I could take a leak behind a tree, so why did I need to pay? He started shouting at me and said he had to pay the municipality one rupee and keep the other rupee for himself. He said he had a large family to support. While he was ranting, I went inside the toilet and could see the man had kept the loo spotlessly clean. When I came out, I gave him a 500-rupee note. He looked amazed and said he didn't have any change. I said: 'Keep it for your family.'

As I was walking away, the man who was screaming at me was now blessing me. Zuni explained why this incident moved her: 'Dad, you realized very quickly he was not shouting at you because he was angry; he was shouting because he was in dire need. He was adamant that he receive two rupees and you gave him 500. What I learnt was if it's within our power to help those in need, we must.'

AJ: We never know how our children will read our actions.

Besides watching movies, what made you happy when you were young? Going on holiday or just playing about?

VVC: In the winter months, we would take the train from Pathankot to Bombay. Of course, we travelled third class. I really looked forward to seeing those beautiful coconut trees lining the tracks as we passed Gujarat. I would stick my neck out of the train window so I could have a better look. I would get so excited when I saw the first coconut tree and then the second one. We didn't have any coconut trees in Kashmir, so somehow I associated the tree with the city of my dreams.

Now when I walk from one house that I own in Pali Hill to the other, I pass a coconut tree. Whenever I see it, I say a prayer and thank the Lord for all my blessings. I have had the coconut tree lit up and can see it from my study when I work there at nights. The tree is a symbol for me and reminds me of those train journeys we made to this city of cinema. I feel so grateful just looking at that tree.

AJ: Now this city of cinema is your home. So tell me how do you relax?

VVC: Working on a script is relaxation for me. There's no stress. I'm making films because I love them. Even when I'm on holiday, I keep thinking of film ideas.

What's most important to me is deciding a film's premise—what is it trying to say? In *Shikara*, I wanted to talk about love and not hate. In *Parinda*, I was trying to say violence begets violence. In *3 Idiots*, it's strive for excellence and success will follow.

AJ: You went back to your origins in *Shikara*. Why did you make that film?

VVC: My mother had come to Bombay in 1989 for the *Parinda* premiere, but she could not return home because at that time thousands of Hindu Pandits had to flee Kashmir. My mother would silently thank the militants because she could now live near me in Bombay and not far away in Kashmir.

I admired the way she chose to look for the good and positive in every situation. That was an important lesson for me. But in the end, she did not want to stay in my house in Bombay and decided to live with my older brother, Vijay, who also had to migrate from Kashmir. She used to say: 'Tu bada khurdara aadmi hai.'

'Khurdara' is rough, you know, like pumice stone. I think she meant: 'You're a rough man. You clean but you hurt.' My mother was a wise lady. [*smiles*]

I wanted to tell her story in *Shikara* through the lives of one couple. It was a very difficult film to make—how do you pitch a story that's so political? What do you do? It was very tough. But I had to make the film no matter the outcome.

AJ: What about the casting?

VVC: Ang Lee once said every film has a god and the god of *Shikara* guided me away from casting stars. I had a very good casting director, Indu Sharma, and told her I wanted real faces—people who had never acted in television or in film before.

Indu saw a photograph of a young girl called Sadia, who was from Bhaderwah, a village in Jammu. Indu auditioned her in Jammu because Sadia's father didn't want her to come to Bombay. He thought this whole audition business was some sort of trick, and that it was not Vidhu Vinod Chopra who wanted her to come to Bombay but some brothel owner trying to lure his daughter. People in small towns are scared that their daughters might be sold off in the big city.

Finally, Sadia's father and I arranged to talk on Facetime. I wore my dark glasses because that's how the media often photographs me—with dark glasses! I spoke in a mix of Kashmiri and Urdu and we chatted for a while. The sweetest moment came when I was saying goodbye to him and he accidentally panned his mobile to his right. And there I was thinking we were having a private conversation on Facetime and in reality the whole mohalla was sitting behind him listening in. [*both laugh*]

AJ: What do you look for in an actor?

VVC: The face, the personality. I look for a certain innocence—it's hard to find because fame and money often corrupt. When I auditioned Sadia, I knew she was exceptional. She reminded me of Nutan, my favourite actress when I was a kid. Sadia has that same innocent face and demeanour.

For Shiv, who was the main character, we needed a voice like Amitabh Bachchan's because Shiv is a poet. Indu Sharma played me a tape of a Bombay radio jockey called Aadil. I loved the sound of his voice and called him in for an audition.

AJ: Are you pleased you went with newcomers? I believe all the heads of department were first-timers too.

VVC: The experience of working with newcomers is so fulfilling that somehow I doubt very much I'll work with established stars again. It's another story that they may not like to work with someone like me. [*both laugh*]

You asked about the crew. Sometimes the crew in popular Hindi cinema get slightly jaded. They've learnt the formula well, they have had to, and when you need a certain shot taken, they can fall into the trap of repeating what they've done before. But I'm looking for innovation and surprise. That's why I went with first-timers. The cameraman, Rangarajan Ramabadran, had never shot a feature film before and neither had Shikhar Misra edited a feature film. I thought, let's get as many new people on board as possible. They'll bring new energy, they'll bring new life to *Shikara.* And I was right.

AJ: What did making the film mean to you?

VVC: I made *Shikara* in memory of my mother. This was our life in Kashmir. When I was growing up, my closest friends were Muslims. My mother used to take me to the temple and to the Hazratbal Shrine. I prayed in both places. I did not know the difference. That was the world I grew up in. That was my India.

The reason I dedicated the film to my mother and Anupama dates back to the time when I was shooting *Broken Horses* in America. Anu was in India and she fell very ill, but did not tell me. She was protecting me. She didn't want me to worry as I was far away in America and I might have wanted to come rushing back despite my shooting schedule. When you love someone, you protect them from suffering. My kids do the same thing. Even my assistant Anuja will avoid telling me something she knows will upset me.

AJ: *Shikara* was released in February 2020 and I'm sure you didn't expect such a huge backlash from the right wing.

VVC: Of course, I didn't. But let's move on. *Shikara* is another story and another book.

AJ: I understand, sir. [*pause*]
  So much time has gone by and you were known to be a pretty fiery person. Would you say you've mellowed over the years?

VVC: I think I have. And that's thanks to Anu. She's the kind of woman who mellows you. My kids are superb. And I believe I have a wonderful relationship with them.

AJ: Quite a different relationship from the one you had with your father.

VVC: Oh my God! Though I loved my father and I'm certain he loved me, I couldn't talk to him as openly as my kids and I talk to each other. We discuss everything. Times have changed.

AJ: Did your father see how well you had done in life?

VVC: He died here in Bombay before *Sazaye Maut* was released. He was no longer there when I made *Khamosh*. He didn't see me well off.

AJ: Do you regret that?

VVC: Very much so. My mother knew I was doing well— that made me happy.

AJ: Did your father believe you would make it?

VVC: I will never know that but I know he was very worried about me. He thought I was mad doing the things I was doing.

I think he wanted me to have a secure and settled life. And that's probably why he wanted me to become a doctor. I told him many times I didn't want to be a doctor but he insisted that I sit for the pre-med exam. I took the exam and got 58 per cent. When my father heard the results, he couldn't believe it. Because I used to do very well at school, he thought there was some clerical mistake and I must have scored 98 per cent and not 58. He asked the college to check the marksheet again but they confirmed there had been no mistake.

I didn't have the courage to tell him that I had answered only three of the six questions. I wanted to make sure that I would get around 50 per cent because I didn't want to be a doctor—I wanted to study film.

AJ: Your father must have been happy about the awards you got for your films, including the Oscar nomination.

VVC: When I spoke to him about the Oscar nomination, I thought it was the perfect moment to admit to him that I had flunked the medical exam on purpose. I thought the nomination would make him happy. So I told him what I had done. He was furious and said:

> How much money is there in an Oscar?
> *Nothing.*
> You're a fool. You'll starve in Bombay. You should have become a doctor. Dr Chopra! Everybody would address you as Doctor Sahib.

It was like that scene in *3 Idiots*! If he were alive today, I think, he would be proud of me. I don't believe I've let him down.

Abhijat, did I ever tell you how much he loved Ghalib? I remember he once recited this Ghalib couplet to me:

> *Dard minnat-kash-e-dava na hua*
> *Main na achcha hua bura na hua*

He asked if I understood the meaning of the lines. I probably wanted to show off and replied:

> The medicine didn't cure me
> I am the same, no worse, no better

My father roared with laughter, which he often did. Though he could lose his temper and get angry and be strict with me, but at heart he was a very kind and gentle person. He explained the idea of the couplet:

> My pain was not beholden to medicine
> I am no better but free of debt

Ghalib's couplet taught me an important lesson. I have never borrowed money from anybody and am in no one's debt. The only person I have taken money from was my brother Vir. Of course, I'm indebted to him and to people like Mr V.S. Shastri and P.K. Nair. They opened the doors to the world of cinema for me.

AJ: You've lived and breathed cinema all your life. Can you tell me if there are some films you could watch again and again?

VVC: *The Godfather* and *8½*. *Citizen Kane* is on my iPad and I keep watching it. I've seen Godard's *Breathless* hundreds of times and Truffaut's *Jules et Jim.* I've also seen *Mughal-e-Azam*, *Pyaasa*, *Navrang*, *Teesri Manzil* and *Mother India* many times. Too many films to count, yaar!

AJ: You have seen many ups and downs in life—but you've also had a lot of success. What does success mean to you?

VVC: It does not mean public acknowledgement or praise from others. Some of the biggest hits that have my name attached to them are not, in my view, my greatest films.

I am sixty-eight and I'm happy to be where I am. The happiness I feel today is how I would define success. I doubt I'll live to be a hundred and if we take the long view, neither success nor failure in the traditional sense will mean anything a hundred years from now. All we have is this moment. Here and now. That's life!

AJ: Before I let you go, can I ask if you have a favourite film among your movies?

VVC: *Shikara* is the film I love the most because it's very close to my heart. As I said, it's a story I made for my mother. It's the story of our family. That's how we grew up at 35A Wazir Bagh, Srinagar, Kashmir.

I remember the day you called me from Ahmedabad and asked if *3 Idiots* was a big hit and I told you: 'Yes, it's huge. I've never seen such box office figures!' And you said: 'While we were writing *3 Idiots* we never imagined it would be as big a hit, did we?' We both laughed. That's what it's all about, Abhijat. When we write a film we never think about whether it'll succeed or not. The day we start thinking about that—it's time for us to hang up our boots.

So many things in this world happen by chance. I'm extremely grateful I was born in Kashmir to parents who were principled and honourable. They were both honest people, incapable of deceit. I could have been born anywhere. I feel indebted and grateful for my life.

It's not always the outcome that matters; the journey is equally important. That reminds me of a couplet by Faiz:

Faiz thi raah sar-ba-sar manzil
Hum jahaan pahunche kaamyaab aaye

[Faiz, the path itself was my destination
Wherever I arrived, I was victorious]

Acknowledgements

I could tell you a lot about creating films, but there was very little I knew about the creation of a book. I found out soon enough that the process is just as intense. For bringing this book to life, I wish to express my gratitude to so many people.

Abhijat Joshi, whose memory is the eighth wonder of the world. It's difficult for me to recall what I had for lunch yesterday, but somehow, he is able to remember incidents from my life when he wasn't even there. Abhijat, this book would have been impossible without you and your splendid mind.

Nasreen Munni Kabir. The manuscript was gathering dust in a cupboard for almost five years. Then, she came into my life, went through the random clutter of innumerable pages, created a structure and gave this book the shape that it now has. Through her editing, she turned a lazy desire into reality.

Anuja Singh, my trusted assistant, for typing all our conversations and turning voice recordings into a manuscript. Smriti Kiran, who kick-started that whole process.

The team at VVC Films—Abhishek Dubey, who had some great ideas that made the reading experience of this book so much better. Rahul Ashta, who dug through thousands of photographs from our collection, some of which you can see in this book. Jaskunwar Kohli, who made more than twenty-five book covers before arriving at the one that has finally become the face of my life's journey. Ramakant Dubey, who has taken care of VVC Films for more than thirty years.

I want to thank Javed Dar, Joy Dutta and Merrick Morton for capturing priceless moments from my film shoots that have eventually made their way into this book.

Thank you, Rahul Nanda, for your creative ideas over the years, and Minakshi Achan, for giving this book a name.

Thank you, Shantanu. Your wisdom in the field of publishing books has been invaluable.

And finally, I thank my parents—for imbibing me with honesty. My brother, Vir, for taking care of me my whole life. Shelly, my sister, it was so much fun to grow up with you. And Subhash Dhar, who is more of a brother than a brother-in-law. My children, Ishaa, Agni and Zuni, and my loving wife, Anupama. If I am happy in this moment, it is because it's full of you.

Thank you everybody.

(VIDHU VINOD CHOPRA)